MIND TRAPS

MIND TRAPS

Change Your Mind
Change Your Life

by Tom Rusk, M.D.
and Natalie Rusk

PRICE STERN SLOAN
Los Angeles

Library of Congress Cataloging-in-Publication Data

Rusk, Tom.
　Mind traps

　Includes index.
　1. Attitude (Psychology)　2. Attitude change.
I. Rusk, Natalie.　II. Title.
BF327.R87　1988　　　　158'.1　　　　　　88-19558
ISBN 0-89596-748-6

Published by Price Stern Sloan, Inc., 360 North La Cienega Boulevard,
Los Angeles, California 90048

ISBN: 0-89586-748-6

To my mother,
who taught me the value of self-respect (and
who would take credit for the book in any case)

To my father,
who taught me how to love

To my wife and children,
who loved me despite my Mind Traps

To my clients,
who have trusted me and had the courage to
experiment with their lives despite my
impatience and unconventional approach

To Jan,
who has been there unobtrusively through it all
and who has helped
more than I can ever repay

And to Randy

ACKNOWLEDGMENTS

I, Tom, am writing this acknowledgment the same way I wrote every other page of this book. First I gave it my best effort, then my daughter, Natalie, displayed her compassion for readers by rewriting it thoroughly. We passed it back and forth in person and by mail from California to Rhode Island and to Taiwan. Then I asked several people I trust for their comments. Finally, Lisa Marsoli and Gina Renée Gross at Price Stern Sloan polished the manuscript into its final form.

We offer heartfelt thanks to all the people who helped us with the book.

In particular, Lisa Marsoli somehow found the time to be an enthusiastic mentor. All authors should be as fortunate with their publishers and editors.

Judy, my wife and Natalie's mother, has provided countless cogent suggestions and offered her patient support over the past three years as we toiled in our *Mind Traps* world.

We also want to thank those who offered so many helpful comments on the text: Nick Erwin, Suzanne Hess, Hannah Lauria, Ellie Leboff, Nancy and Steve Smith, Dr. Steve Solomon, Lilian Vineberg and Dr. Yanon Volcani.

MIND TRAP LIST

The Self-Doubt Trap:

"I have doubts about myself. I'm afraid there may be something wrong with me."

The Feelings Traps

The "Bad Feelings Are Wrong" Trap:

"When I'm unhappy it's difficult to feel good about myself. Uncomfortable feelings (such as anger, hurt, resentment and embarrassment) make me wonder what's wrong with me."

The "Feelings Are Foolish" Trap:

"Strong feelings are messy and unreasonable. It's unfortunate to have them, worse to show them and useless to discuss them. To stay in control of my life I need to control my feelings."

The Fear of Change Traps

The "Biased Against Myself" Traps:

The Compare and Despair Trap: "When I compare myself to others I usually come out the loser. They're as good as they seem; I'm as bad as I feel."

The "You Flatter Me" Trap: "Thanks for the compliment, but I'm afraid you're mistaken. You don't know me the way I do."

The "People Don't Change" Traps:

The "I Can't Change" Trap: "I am who I've always believed I am and there's no use trying to be different."

The "You'll Never Change" Trap: "I know you're trying to change, but I'm afraid to be hopeful. You seem so awkward and phony when you try to be different. I know sooner or later you'll go back to the way you were."

The "Seen One, Seen 'Em All" Trap: "My experience proves that all men/women are alike. I know they'll disappoint me in the long run. There's no sense getting to close."

The Fear of Failure and Responsibility Traps

The Fear of Failure and Success Traps:

The Fear of Failure Trap: "If I try, I'll probably fail. So why try? It's better to die a potential winner than a proven loser."

The Fear of Success Trap: "Success builds expectations and makes disappointment worse when I fail. It's safer not to try too hard, get too good or have too much fun, love and success."

The "There's No Use Trying" Trap:

Stuck Without Choices: "I have to be where I am, with the person I'm with, doing what I'm doing—even though I don't really want to be."

Pessimism: "It's futile. No matter how well things are going, I know something will happen to ruin it. When something bad happens, it's evidence that things never work out in the long run. If something good happens, it means I just got lucky."

Cynicism: "Nothing I or anyone else does makes any real difference."

"It's Too Late": "What's the use of trying to change? I've already wasted too much time and I'd probably fail anyway. If I somehow were to become successful, I'd hate myself for not having started earlier."

Boredom: "Nothing interests me. I don't have anything valuable to offer the world and the world doesn't have anything to offer me."

The Blame Trap

"I Blame Myself": "I keep screwing up and ruining everything. There must be something wrong with me."

"I Blame Others (or Fate or God)": "My difficulties aren't my fault."

The "My Happiness Is Your Responsibility" Traps:

The Dependency Trap: "I have to rely on someone else to make decisions. I can't trust my own thoughts, feeling and judgments."

The "Love Me And Make Me Whole" Trap: "If no one is committed to me, it must mean something is wrong with me. Everything would be fine if only someone would give me the love I've always wanted but never had."

The Complacent Partner Trap: "Now that I've got someone, I can take him or her for granted. I no longer have to take care of myself."

The Searching For the Perfect Love Trap: "No one I've met is good enough. I'll just keep looking for someone who'll give me the love I need to make me feel whole."

The Fear of Rejection Traps

The Rejection Trap:

"Less Intimacy, Less Pain": "I can't trust you enough to get too close. I'm afraid you'll end up leaving me and I'll be so hurt I won't be able to handle it. The less I open myself up to you, the better."

"Better to Reject Than Be Rejected": I'm so afraid I'll be rejected. I'd better get what I can from you and then find some excuse to reject you before I get too committed, vulnerable and hurt.

Control the News: "I'm afraid no one would care about me if they knew what I really thought and felt. I don't want to burden you, hurt you or lose you, so I'd better only reveal what won't upset you."

The Jealousy Trap:

"I'm afraid you'll leave me for someone else. I want to know everything you do while you're away from me. My jealousy proves how much I love you."

The Shy and Lonely Trap:

Shyness: "People can see right through me and can tell there's something wrong with me. The more I admire people, the more awkward I become. If I hide how I think and feel, others are less likely to discover my inadequacies."

"Only Losers Are Lonely": "I'm lonely. No one really cares about me. Other people have good friends and loving partners. There must be something wrong with me."

The Prove Your Worth Traps

The Great American Success Trap:

Prior To Success: "If I were successful, I'd no longer doubt myself. I'd feel worthwhile, fulfilled and happy. It makes sense to put success ahead of everything else."

After Success: "According to everyone else I'm successful. Why don't I feel worthwhile, fulfilled and happy? There must be something wrong with me."

The Perfectionism Trap:

"Maybe I can prove I'm not a bad person by becoming perfect or as close to it as possible."

The Conceit Trap:

"As long as I keep reminding everyone that I've got more going for me than most people, I don't have to worry about not being good enough."

The "I'm Right and You're Wrong" Trap:

"Only one of us can be right—either I'm right and you're wrong or (God forbid) you're right and I'm wrong. Being wrong about something makes me feel something is wrong with me."

The "Your Happiness Is My Responsibility" Trap:

"I feel like I should take care of anyone who is unhappy. I have trouble saying no, regardless of what I really think, feel and want."

TABLE OF CONTENTS

Part 9:
The Self-Change Program

Appendix

INTRODUCTION

What are Mind Traps? Mind Traps are self-defeating attitudes. Mind Traps keep people stuck in familiar ruts.

This book asks you to stand back from yourself and consider the possibility that habitual attitudes may be getting in your way. *Mind Traps* is designed to help you identify those attitudes and escape them.

I once promised myself I would never write another self-help book. I had more I wanted to say, but surely there were too many of these books on the shelves already. Then I realized that every book ever written could be classified as self-help. From the *Bible* to *War and Peace*, from *The Joy of Cooking* to *Origin of the Species*, everything is written and read to improve life in some way.

Mind Traps has no pretensions about being great literature. It is intended as a practical guide. It addresses those readers who are interested in the most noble of human endeavors: the pursuit of self-understanding and personal change. *Mind Traps* offers a new approach to this challenging enterprise.

The book describes the major Mind Traps that interfere with people's lives and suggests an Escape Route for each trap. Escape Routes are healthier attitudes you can adopt if you want to change.

Feelings are the key to personal change. Part 4 of *Mind Traps* provides a guide to understanding and using specific feelings.

Part 4 is a *Self-Change Program* for those readers who are determined to escape from Mind Traps and improve their lives. You may choose to begin *Mind Traps* by reading this part first. The *Self-Change Program* proposes an ideal of well-being to help readers set goals for self-change. This ideal can help you clarify what may be missing in your life. The program goes on to delineate an attitude conducive to self-change. The final chapter presents step-by-step directions for using the book to help you grow.

The Appendix includes a glossary, an index and a note to therapists entitled, *Helping People Help Themselves.*

Mind Traps is filled with examples from my struggle to overcome my own Mind Traps and from my clinical experience.

I wish you courage. I've tried to provide everything else you'll need to change to a better life.

MIND TRAPS

PART 1

An Introduction to Self-Doubt and Mind Traps

CHAPTER 1

Self-Doubt and Mind Traps

> **"I wouldn't belong to a club that would have me as a member."**
>
> > attributed to Groucho Marx
> > by Woody Allen

> **"If you really got to know me, you wouldn't want to know me."**
>
> > from *Jacques and His Master*
> > by Milan Kundera

Self-Doubt: A Portrait of the Author

I remember some years ago sitting on the toilet in a dark bathroom, weeping as quietly as I could. I pounded at my temples in a vain attempt to distract myself from what I was feeling.

My wife, Judy, slept peacefully in bed on the other side of the bathroom door. The infuriating sound of her deep, regular breathing had driven me to my humiliating refuge. I could no longer endure lying beside her. I felt too isolated, too lonely, too sorry for myself.

I had been awake in bed for what seemed like hours. I had wanted her to wake up and comfort me. Yet, at the same time, I had tried to avoid the slightest movement, lest our bodies touch, lest I disturb her and give her the satisfaction of believing I felt close to her, lest I betray my craving to be held like a child while I cried in her arms. To get the comforting I wanted by asking for it, by admitting my need, would have been worse than getting none at all! It would have felt meaningless and humiliating.

I worried that I might go crazy if I couldn't get myself to feel better. But I didn't know what to do. I couldn't see any way out of my dilemma.

Earlier that day while I drove the car pool, Scott, our oldest child, had made fun of me in front of his sister and their friends:

"Way to go, Dad. You did it again. You're going the wrong way. Don't you remember anything? We never pick up Sally on Wednesdays. My Dad never knows where he's going. Do you, Dad?"

I said nothing, but I fumed. I silently vowed not to do to Scott what he was doing to me. Instead I would tear into him in private, away from the others. I relished the thought of it, rehearsing my harangue as I drove them to school, late as usual.

But he was right and I knew it. Absent-mindedness was, and still is, I'm afraid, one of my trademarks. Yet I thought that was no excuse for his insulting disrespect, although it was typical of what I experienced on a daily basis in our home.

That evening, I moped at the dinner table. I refused to respond honestly to my family's compassionate questions.

"What's up, Dad? Problems at the clinic?"

"No, everything's fine." My monotone lie convinced no one. It wasn't meant to.

Judy escalated to sarcasm:

"You certainly know how to make dinner a happy family time!"

I was recalling all this later that night while sitting on my humble throne. What was wrong with me and my life? I tried to reassure myself with a desperate hope: Maybe my unhappiness wasn't my fault.

I wanted to blame Judy. She was leading the way, setting a bad example for the kids. I constructed what I hoped would be an overwhelming and incontestable argument I could use to confront, accuse and humiliate her. I indulged myself with a melodramatic fantasy in which she would admit the error of her ways and capitulate, groveling before me in guilt and self-castigation:

> Tom, please forgive me for not admiring, complimenting, and respecting you—my brilliant and strong husband, loving father of our children, outstanding psychiatrist, distinguished professor, innovative administrator and excellent provider for the family. I'll change my ways. I'll treat you with respect and I'll hug and kiss you at every opportunity. I'll make you happy—I promise!

An ironic fantasy because, unfortunately, I couldn't accept the very thing I wished she would believe about me—that I was a good person who deserved respect and happiness.

The Familiar & False Self-Doubting Self

Like everyone else, I grew up believing I was who I thought myself to be. Everyone has a self-concept, a familiar and habitual sense of who his or her "I" is—separate and different from others and the world.

Stand back and consider yourself. Are you merely and

actually the person you believe yourself to be? I suggest that the self you believe is the real you is not. Who you think you are is neither your only nor necessarily your best option. If you're like most people, it is difficult for you to see yourself in as favorable a light as those who know you do. The familiar, habitual "I" that you accept as genuine always takes you on a detour from your true self.

It is exceedingly difficult to appreciate that *the only lens you've ever looked through may be distorting your perspective.* And, as you'll see in later chapters, it is frightening to think you may be wrong about yourself. It is disturbing to realize you may not know who you really are and could be. I now realize that the self I believed in was my familiar but false, self-doubting self. I trusted that I was the person I had always known myself to be, but I had little confidence *in* myself.

As a child I was considered to be, and thought of myself as, fat, spoiled and lazy. There I was in the bathroom at thirty-three, demoralized, blubbering and lonely. I still thought of myself as fat, flawed and inadequate. I sensed that deep within me something was terribly wrong.

By then I had been at approximately normal weight for years, I had placed near the top of my medical school class, I was an associate professor at the University of California, San Diego, and received an outstanding teacher award on two occasions, I was working eighty hours a week as director of the crisis clinic I had originated, I had been married for over a decade and had three fine children.

I was one of a vast army of people with their fair share of inherited talents who are nonetheless plagued by insecurities about themselves. I had unconsciously hoped to erase my self-doubt by working as hard as I could to prove my worth. I was trying to impress others and compensate for my lifelong reservations about myself.

My self-doubt was so disconcerting I couldn't stand to be alone with my thoughts and my feelings about myself. I relied on continuous frenetic activity to distract myself. I was never relaxed and carefree. Whether by wisecracking or pontificating, I sought to be center stage. I needed the constant reassurance of others' rapt interest.

Though no longer obese, I was out of condition. I rarely took time for leisure or exercise, except occasionally with our children.

Weekend after weekend I would silently mope around my effervescent family, resenting them for their good humor. But let the phone ring and I would cheerfully chat with the caller while my family watched in pained dismay at my transformation. What else could they believe but that I was angry and upset with them for something they were doing wrong—or worse, that I didn't love them or want to be around them.

Many people regard their immediate families as extensions of themselves and treat them accordingly. If you have significant self-doubt, you probably treat your family as badly as you treat yourself. Meanwhile, you may give friends, acquaintances and even complete strangers the best you have to offer. It's as if you expect those closest to you to share your misery, but want those outside the family circle to think well of you. (Many philanthropists and humanitarians reputedly have been hell to live with.)

Although I didn't realize it at the time, I was suffering from burn-out as a result of my workaholic attempts to prove myself. I was stuck in *The Self-Doubt Trap* (Chapter 4), the most basic Mind Trap, and *The Great American Success Trap* (Chapter 19). I felt flawed and undeserving of the understanding my family would have been happy to give me. I was in my own way. I was preventing myself from receiving the comfort and support I was starving for.

I wasn't standing back from myself and my situation. I lacked any compassion for my own pain. I saw my pain as evidence of my defectiveness. I believed that to feel so bad must be evidence that something was wrong with me. This confusion between feeling hurt and being flawed is widespread and disabling (*The "Bad Feelings Are Wrong" Trap*—Chapter 6).

Even my wife and closest friends didn't realize how inadequate and flawed I sensed I was or how much I hurt. I was embarrassed by what others might think of me if they discovered how frightened, lonely and weak I felt behind my assertive and confident mask. As a result, I couldn't accept the compliments people gave me.

I would waste my time and energy looking around me and selecting people with whom I could compare myself unfavorably. I would choose only those who had characteristics I envied, those who seemed to be what I believed I was not. This was my private, self-flagellating, no-win game—a torture to which I had subjected myself ever since grade school. Most people seemed more spontaneous, carefree and confident than I was—this is *The Compare and Despair Trap* (Chapter 11).

No one except my wife suspected my many fears, especially my fears about success and failure. I was afraid that failure would confirm my worst fears about myself— that I was indeed defective. If I succeeded, that would merely increase others' expectations of me and make their disappointment all the worse when the inevitable happened and I ultimately did fail. So I was also caught in *The Fear of Failure and Success Traps* (Chapter 13).

Yet I wanted to prove my worth by becoming successful. Behind clouds of self-doubt hides the shining hope of redemption. I was afraid to try and fail, afraid that failure would prove I was worthless. Yet I was driven to excel so that everyone, including myself, would be convinced I was valuable. I was like a pinball ricocheting between my Mind Traps, the distorted attitudes created by my self-doubt.

Self-doubt is disturbing, but a sense of worthlessness is terrifying. Self-doubt provides a degree of protection from what would otherwise be a devastating sense of defectiveness and despair. Better to doubt one's worth than to be convinced one is worthless. Doubt at least offers hope of eventually feeling worthwhile.

Mind Traps are self-defeating attitudes generated by self-doubt. They serve two contradictory, fear-reducing functions:

1) One type of Mind Trap is *The Compensatory Mind Trap.* Compensatory Mind Traps are attempts to reassure yourself that you are not indelibly flawed. These Mind Traps prevent self-doubt from growing into a feeling of worthlessness. One example is an obsessive pursuit of success. Conceit is another way of compensating for the fear that something may be wrong with you.

2) The other major kind of self-defeating attitude is *The Familiarity Mind Trap.* Familiarity Traps are attempts to stay the way you are. Even if you are filled with self-doubt, you will be afraid to change because if you do, you will lose your familiar identity. It's terrifying to not know who you are. The purpose of this set of Mind Traps is to reassure yourself that you are who you have always believed yourself to be. Examples of Familiarity Traps include a tendency to compare oneself unfavorably with others, difficulty believing honest compliments, and a reluctance to work at anything with enthusiasm.

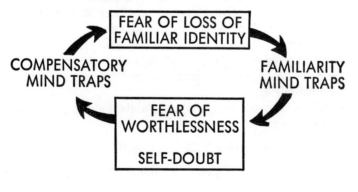

The fear of feeling worthless and the fear of losing one's familiar identity act as opposing forces. You may sense this struggle within yourself. The confusion caused by trying to prove your worth and at the same time trying to hold onto your familiar, negative sense of yourself may even increase your self-doubt and multiply your Mind Traps.

Compensatory and Familiarity Mind Traps can drive you to try to prove you are good at something and yet refuse to believe it when you succeed. A typical example of someone with this conflict is a diligent student who panics before an exam, receives her usual "A" and then explains away her success saying, "I'm not that smart. The grading was easy and they just happened to ask the questions I had prepared for."

This cycle of self-doubt interacting with Mind Traps can keep you going in circles throughout your entire life unless you learn how to make the leap of faith in yourself necessary to accept your worth. But as you will soon see, this leap to self-acceptance is readily accomplished by a series of small courageous steps, each based on self-respect generating actions and compassion for yourself and others.

Who Suffers From Self-Doubt

Many people are chronically frustrated. They sense they're not getting enough out of life. They want to change but they're stuck because they're oblivious to the source of their dilemma and painfully unaware how much time and effort they waste dealing with self-doubt. They're blind to their self-doubt, the lifelong misunderstanding at the root of their dissatisfaction.

People who are stuck tend to have the following thoughts and attitudes:

- "I'm unhappy with my life and myself."

- "It's wrong to feel some of the things I feel."

- "I'm lonely. What's wrong with me?"

- "Other people often have a higher opinion of me than I do."

- "I keep choosing friends and lovers who aren't good for me."

- "I know I'm a jealous person, but I can't help it."

- "I don't trust myself to make good decisions."

- "I can't commit myself wholeheartedly to anything."

- "Despite my accomplishments, I don't feel fulfilled."

- "I feel like a failure."

- "I'm shy and self-conscious."

- "Other people are better at what they do than I am."

Do some of these sound familiar? All of the above attitudes suggest self-doubt. You may be aware of having one of these attitudes and yet not have identified it as evidence of self-doubt.

Most people have self-doubt. They may feel it acutely or merely as a gnawing discomfort. Self-doubt is so widespread, it tends to be taken for granted. It's virtually impossible to grow up without it.

Some people dwell on their insecurity about themselves. Others try to deny it. Some hide their self-doubt, others talk about it endlessly. Some people even use self-doubt as a way of introducing themselves, offering it to strangers like a handshake. These people deprecate themselves to disarm others and protect themselves, as if to say, "I'm screwed up so you don't have to feel threatened by me. If I admit that you're better, maybe you'll accept me as your inferior. Even if you don't and reject me, at least I'm prepared for it."

As you'll soon see, you are making a serious mistake if you assume that just because self-doubt is so common it must be of little significance, something one must learn to live with—the athlete's foot or dandruff of the mind.

People with self-doubt adopt all sorts of attitudes to manage their fears about themselves depending on the situation. If you suffer from self-doubt, you either assume your fears of inadequacy are depressingly valid, exhaust yourself trying to prove your worth and reassure yourself, or run from feelings of inadequacy, blaming whomever and whatever is handy for your unhappiness. These self-defeating attitudes are Mind Traps. Mind Traps prevent you from achieving fulfillment and well-being.

Self-Doubt: Summary

Your self-doubt doesn't feel foreign. Imbedded in your personality, self-doubt affects your beliefs about specific aspects of yourself; because of self-doubt you may have doubts about your appearance, your intelligence and your abilities. Many talented and bright people are dissatisfied with themselves. When others compliment them on their talents, they feel uncomfortable and attempt to explain away the evidence. You may be one of these gifted but insecure people.

The effects of self-doubt go far deeper than an inability to accept one's talents and attributes. Self-doubt is a mental abscess which can penetrate to the very essence of your being. Like a slow-growing but highly adaptable fungus, self-doubt is a creeping rot which eats away at your sense of worth. It can be so insidious you may be unaware of its damaging effect on your life. And self-doubt is extremely durable; it is resistant to all but the most sophisticated and determined efforts at eradicating it.

Introduced by painful experiences in childhood, self-doubt weaves itself into the fabric of your identity. There, disguised as the truth, utilizing the self-defeating attitudes (Mind Traps) it generates, self-doubt asserts its poisonous influence over every aspect of life, from work to relationships. Self-doubt and Mind Traps are hardy enough to withstand overwhelming conflicting evidence. They are even resistant to good common sense—no matter how much some people may love and respect you, you may still doubt yourself. And you may find yourself sabotaging your own welfare.

CHAPTER 2

The Origin of Self-Doubt

"My apprehensions come in crowds;
I dread the rustling of the grass;
The very shadows of the clouds
Have power to shake me as they pass:
I question things and do not find
One that will answer to my mind;
And all the world appears unkind."

William Wordsworth

Childhood Pain: Too Much of the Wrong Stuff

"Are you sure you're not a girl? You've got more to show than my sister. Hey, come over here you guys. Look at his boobs!"

This scene was the living nightmare of my youth—the danger I risked each time I removed my shirt and revealed my naked obesity. As a child, I seemed to have too much of everything. I grew up in a working class neighborhood in Montreal, Canada. We lived on the top floor of a brick building which housed our family's bakery. I had every material thing a child could want, and more cake than even I could consume. I was a waddling advertisement for our eclectic bakery products: cakes and pies, kosher-style breads, imitation French pastries, and Jewish High Holiday specialties. Our family was well-known. Loyal customers would drive miles from posh neighborhoods to shop at our bakery.

I was the fattest, the richest and the only Jewish kid (besides my older brother) within a fifteen-block radius. My brother and I paid a price for our family's notoriety. He refused to be intimidated and would be beaten up repeatedly. I remember one day when I was in first grade I emerged from school and saw two hooligans tormenting him. One pinned my brother down while the other wrote "JEW BOY" on his face in indelible ink. By heaving a brick which narrowly missed their heads, I made them run away (and earned the reputation of "that crazy fat kid").

I avoided my brother's fate by stealing from our bakery and buying off the local bullies with pies and cakes. I would sneak into the back of the bakery, squeeze my ample body between the racks, secretly stuff the fattening loot under my jacket and make a quick getaway.

Soon I had many friends. ("Let them eat cake" worked better for me than for Marie Antoinette.) But deep down I knew I was defective—fat, weird, half-boy half-girl, Jewish and a thief, with friends only because I bribed them.

In junior high school, I used every trick I could think of to avoid gym classes. I dreaded undressing and showering in front of the others.

"Rusk, why aren't you ready?" the gym teacher demanded.

"I couldn't get shorts in my size, sir," was my feeble, humiliating lie.

"Try Abdullah-the-Tentmaker," he suggested sneering, evoking peals of laughter from my classmates.

By the time I was a teenager, my parents were aware I had problems. They loved me and couldn't bear to see me in pain. They tried to protect me by intervening on my behalf. They made excuses for me to teachers and camp counselors. I tried to avoid any situation that placed demands on me, any situation where I might fail or be embarrassed. And I could count on my parents to intercede and protect me.

My parents and I never sat down and talked about how I felt. I suppose they wanted to avoid the discomfort of a discussion. Deep inside I believed even they were ashamed of who I was. I hated myself for my defects and my cowardice, and I resented my parents for producing a freak and validating my sense of inadequacy by helping me hide.

My childhood wasn't uniformly painful. I was an above-average athlete despite my weight. People would often laugh at my jokes. But my fear of being revealed as abnormal, cowardly and defective was constantly with me. No one understood. No one could comfort me. I was alone with my unhappiness, but I didn't know how lonely I was. It was the only life I knew.

Self-Doubt and Childhood Pain

I believe my unhappiness and loneliness was not unusual. Many children suffer far more than I did with much less support from the people around them. Most adults had more emotional pain in childhood than they care to recall or admit. Some children suffer more than others, but no childhood is free of pain.

A comic strip I saw recently shows a father saying to his son, "Cheer up, kid. These are the happiest years of your life." The child replies with astonishment, "You mean it gets worse?!"

Childhood is often depicted as a carefree time in life.

This is a lie. Childhood is inevitably painful. And lifelong self-doubt is caused by uncomforted childhood pain.

Few adults, even those with the best of intentions, can accurately remember and therefore fully appreciate what it feels like to be a child. Childhood is arguably the most difficult time most people ever encounter. Conceived and born without their consent, ready or not, children must grow up and face life's difficult challenges.

Highly evolved consciousness makes humans' burdens greater than those of other creatures. Only we anticipate our own deaths. We alone are forced to make choices influenced by shame, guilt, and self-respect. Only we worry about the possibility of an afterlife, the origin and end of the universe.[1] And it is as children that we must begin to confront these dilemmas.

At five years of age, Carl, our youngest son, bitterly confronted me and my wife. He had just seen a pile of dead bodies in Vietnam on the TV news. Through tears of anguish he demanded confirmation of his worst fear: "I'm going to die!"

Judy and I looked helplessly at each other, not knowing what to say. Finally I tried to help, "Yes, Carl, but not for a very long time. Look how old we are and we still have lots of time left."

Carl was not consoled. "If you knew I had to die, why did you have me?" he asked.

He had seen through our lame reassurances. (Intelligence, like any inborn gift, can be advantageous. But talents also increase the vulnerability of those who possess them. Gifts are burdens, too.)

When we discussed this episode much later with Scott, our oldest son, he commented, "Yeah, I felt the same thing, but I never said anything. I just had trouble falling asleep

---

[1]*Although there is no way I can prove that only humans ruminate about such issues, other animals are certainly in a poor position to argue with me.*

for a few years." Although different children may handle fear and unhappiness in different ways, each must face the harsh realities of life.

Childhood is the most vulnerable time in life. In childhood, people have the least experience and perspective, yet feelings are at their maximum intensity. A frenzied, red, writhing infant emits heart-rending wails merely because he or she is hungry. A sharp word is enough to start a child crying. In adolescence, just holding hands with your date can be absolutely electrifying. Acute sensitivity during childhood makes each hurt all the more painful and each fear all the more frightening.

Self-Doubt and Loneliness

Children get far more attention for their actions than understanding and comfort for their feelings. As a result, they often feel isolated and lonely. Children take their emotional discomfort personally—especially when their pain is endured alone. If their pain remains uncomforted and unacknowledged, children will end up blaming themselves for how bad they feel.

Physically abused children are convinced they are somehow bad. What else can they believe, having received punishment when what they craved was understanding and support? Abused children always feel defective.

However, blaming parents is unjust and useless. My profession, psychiatry, has received some warranted criticism for fostering this prejudice against parents and especially mothers. The vast majority of parents have always done the best they could, given their beliefs and circumstances.

One of my self-doubting clients used to idealize his childhood. Later he recalled his mother jabbing him with a fork to remind him of proper table manners and rubbing his nose in his soiled undershorts when he would have an "accident." To blame his mother now for her actions would solve nothing, but if he was ever going to give up his self-doubt and accept himself, he had to learn to feel compassion for the young boy inside him who had experienced the hurt and loneliness.

To overcome self-doubt two extremes must be avoided: idealizing parents while denying one's true feelings and resenting parents for how they were. The challenge, especially for those of us who had very little comforting as children, is to learn to feel compassion for the needy, lonely and wounded child in our past who lives within us for the rest of our lives. Recognition of and compassion for the uncomforted hurt we experienced as children can help us move from self-doubt to self-acceptance.

Childhood pain endured alone is where, how and when self-doubt begins. And the brighter and more sensitive the child, the more likely it is that child will suffer pain and, therefore, self-doubt.

Self-Doubt and Human Misery

Self-doubt is the basis of human maliciousness toward self and others. It is not merely a side effect. It is fundamental. *Self-doubt is the root of all meanness and evil.*

Self-doubt is the reason people resort to the extremes of homicide or suicide. It is part of the cause for alcoholism, drug abuse and eating disorders. Because of self-doubt, people waste time being lonely and miserable despite their otherwise manifest good fortune.

The childhood origin of self-doubt is always the same—a child feels deeply hurt repeatedly. Over time, the pain and seething resentment boil over and sear the child's fragile core; insufficient understanding and comforting creates a permanent wound. No adult explains to the child that, unfortunately, *pain is part of life and not punishment for personal flaws.*

Children mistake hurt as evidence they are flawed. Pain

---

is a message from the spirit indicating it has been wounded. Children misunderstand their hurt and become alienated from their spirits. The core part of the child—the spirit, the true self, the vulnerable child within—becomes buried in the attempt to avoid further pain and fear of personal defectiveness. For the lonely child who lacks comforting and understanding, to have pain means to feel wrong and bad.

In this confusion of *feeling bad* with *being bad,* a tragic misunderstanding about the self takes root and begins to distort every aspect of life. The belief that there is something wrong with the self may not prevent accomplishment, but it will always preclude a feeling of fulfillment in work and intimacy in relationships. The feeling of defectiveness makes a sense of well-being impossible.

Alienation from one's true self continues into adult life. Amorphous confusion about oneself slowly matures, hardening into a permanent lens of self-doubt and distrust of others. This distorting lens becomes a core part of the child's, and later the adult's, sense of identity.

Over the years, as a psychiatric consultant to the courts, I have studied the childhoods of more than two dozen murderers. Without exception, they suffered severe physical and emotional abuse during childhood. One man who had killed several women and children had been brutally beaten repeatedly by his father and occasionally by his mother during his childhood.

Read any detailed account of the life histories of notorious villains such as Charles Manson and Adolf Hitler and you will find overwhelming evidence of abuse in childhood.[2] Although we may hate to acknowledge it, the Mansons and Hitlers of the world were once like all the rest

---

[2] *Alice Miller's superb book about physical and psychological child abuse and its lifelong effects,* For Your Own Good, *analyzes the evidence of abuse in Adolf Hitler's childhood. She offers a fascinating speculation: If Hitler had had children early in his adult life might he have abused them and been satisfied with that? Might millions of people have been spared?*

of us: vulnerable children at the mercy of their elders. *Every extreme evil-doer was abused as a child.* Although this realization does not excuse their behavior, it may help explain it and perhaps raise our consciousness about how we treat children.

People who have absorbed too much pain for too long during childhood are those most likely to harbor the terror of worthlessness. Their wounds feel like defects. In a futile attempt to escape the fear of defectiveness, these emotional invalids may displace their self-hatred onto others.

When animals are hurt they try to escape or attack. Humans are no different, just more sophisticated and diverse in our methods. People who have been repeatedly threatened and injured develop their own unique and habitual styles of escape and attack. Their destructive behavior toward themselves and others reveals how inadequately they were comforted and respected during childhood. Being loving and considerate feels alien to people who have spent their lives feeling hurt, angry and bad.

Although people with self-hatred are at the extreme, everyone finds it difficult to act in unfamiliar ways for any length of time. People keep doing what they are accustomed to and what fits their sense of themselves. *People exhibit in their actions their most profound beliefs about themselves.* Behaving with self-respect would feel incongruous to people filled with self-hatred.

Villainy and self-hatred can result from extreme abuse. Milder emotional deprivation is the rule in most people's childhoods and self-doubt, not self-hatred, is the most common result. But self-doubt alone is sufficient to produce serious and unnecessary obstacles in your life.

Prevention of Self-Doubt: Comforting

Childhood discomfort can't be avoided, but the development of self-doubt can be minimized. Part of the secret to preventing self-doubt is for caretakers to increase the comforting they provide children.

Sincere, tender commiseration buffers pain. When generously offered and genuinely accepted, comfort functions as a shock absorber to smooth life's jarring ride.

Do you remember being hugged and comforted as a child when your feelings were hurt? Being comforted by someone bigger and older helps children realize that *their pain isn't their fault.* Life is frequently and unavoidably painful. *No one is intrinsically flawed.*

Compassionate parents can help their children by letting them know:

> We love you and feel bad that you feel hurt and unhappy. We wish we could prevent any pain you may feel, but we can't. The best we can do is to hold you, to try to understand, to care and to help you realize you are not alone.

Comforting doesn't produce weakness—quite the opposite. Comforting makes people resilient to the blows of fate. It is overprotection, neglect and abuse that breed self-doubt, which in turn creates cowardice, prejudice and malice. To borrow from the world of computers: Garbage in, garbage out—an ugly phrase for an ugly phenomenon.

Consider your own childhood. Do you recall having received comforting when you were upset? Was there someone who was sensitive to what you were feeling? Was there at least one consoling adult to hold you in her or his arms while you cried, yet not suffocate you with overprotection?

Weren't you most hurt and lonely when your parents lost their temper and vented their anger at you? After the explosion, when their anger waned, did they ever come back to reassure you about their love for you and your worth?

One of my clients remembers returning from school one afternoon crying, bruised and dirty after being beaten up by neighborhood kids. His father came home in response to his mother's frantic call and proceeded to whip him for being a crybaby. That evening they dragged him to the local YMCA and enrolled him in a boxing class. This episode was typical of their insensitivity to their son's feelings. He grew up to become a lonely, insecure workaholic physician who drank too much and hid his vulnerability behind an unpredictable and violent temper.

If you have self-doubt, then you weren't sufficiently comforted during childhood. If you aren't able to recall needing or receiving physical affection and sensitive understanding during your childhood, it's likely that your family's atmosphere encouraged you to handle your discomfort as best you could *on your own.* In many families the implicit message is: "Let's be happy (or pretend we are) so we don't upset one another." If this family message reminds you of your own, the odds are high that you grew up doubting your inherent worth.

Prevention of Self-Doubt: Respect

Comforting helps prevent self-doubt, but comforting alone isn't enough. Children must be given respect for their capacity to learn from experience, *including painful experience.* There can be no more difficult prescription for a loving parent to follow than this: *Children must not be overprotected.*

Overprotection, however well-intentioned, implies that parents have little faith in their child's ability to learn to handle a situation or master a skill. Overprotection protects parents and damages children. Children should be allowed to try and occasionally fail, to get hurt and then be comforted. Parents need to resist overprotection while appreciating a child's need to be comforted when in pain.

Overprotection is smothering and disrespectful. Instead of trying to protect children from being hurt by constraining them with rules and prohibitions, why not shift strategies and express concerns. When our adolescent children start demanding more independence and freedom, why not ask them to assure us in their words and actions that they can handle the responsibility?

If our children want more autonomy, it's up to them to demonstrate their willingness and capacity to take care of themselves. If children are obviously taking good care of themselves, it relieves parents of some of the responsibility of trying to protect and control them. By giving them responsibility for themselves, everyone is better off.

I once consulted with a family who was paying the price of having exerted excessive control over their children. The parents had kept their children on a tight leash out of love and concern for the children's well-being. As young adults, all three were haunted with severe self-doubt and almost entirely dependent on their parents for their decisions and finances.

A crisis erupted when their son, who was only perfunctorily attending college, informed them that he was considering taking up hang gliding, paying for it with the money they had given him to support himself in school. They called me in a panic, asking how they could go about preventing him from participating in such a perilous activity.

The son explained to me that he felt suffocated by his parents' unsolicited and unrelenting advice in every aspect of his life. He recalled being punished severely for getting into a fight as a child. They ordered him never to fight again. Physical combat was dangerous, unnecessary and inappropriate, they explained. He told me he had recently begun to fantasize getting involved in risky and unethical activities like selling illegal drugs. He said it was the only way he could feel challenged and successful at something his parents hadn't urged him to do!

Earlier I referred to another father who severely punished his son for not fighting. Here were parents demanding the exact opposite. Neither set of parents had faith in their child's ability to make his own decisions. Why don't parents simply express their loving concerns and values but understand that children must learn from experience how to live their own lives?

If parents insist on having veto power over their child's friends, classes and activities, the child will grow up to be insecure. Raised with conventional, protective "limit-setting," a child will grow up to be either passively obedient to others' authority or defiantly rebellious. If a child isn't trusted to take care of herself, she will never learn to be responsible for and concerned about her own well-being.

What if your parents had used a more respectful, but less conventional, approach to raising you? Imagine that they had let you know how concerned they were about your study habits and your choice of friends, yet allowed you to make your own decisions and offered comfort when you had to face the consequences of your errors—like having to repeat the school year or being betrayed by your so-called friends. This unconventional approach to parenting is far more demanding of parents and children. But it works, and for good reasons (and I have the evidence of three self-accepting, responsible and loving adult children to back it up). Children will develop a sense of personal responsibility and confidence if they are allowed to succeed and fail on their own with a loving adult nearby to express fear and concern openly, to encourage them, to applaud their successes and to comfort them when they fail. Of course, children must also learn that respect and comfort have to flow both ways. Parents have feelings, too.

Learning about Comforting

Why don't people accept more comforting for life's burdens? Why do so many lead lives of lonely desperation?

Human beings must learn to be comforted. Each person has an inborn capacity to be nurtured and to nurture others. But this capacity won't develop without training and exposure to comforting adults during childhood. Everyone has a different capacity and need for comforting. Even plants of the same species have different requirements for light, food and water.

If children are smothered with overprotection or ignored, if they are not understood and comforted for what they are feeling, if they are not given the amount of caring and support that fits their individual needs—then their ability to provide and receive tenderness will wither and their sense of worth will deteriorate along with it.

If you didn't receive enough support for your feelings in childhood, you will find comforting hard to accept in adulthood. As a result, you may have difficulty comforting your partner or children. Emotionally deprived children often become emotionally depriving parents.

But not inevitably. Some ignored and abused children grow up to be loving adults. Many insufficiently comforted children grow up to be health care professionals and child care workers. Yet their own capacity to accept affection and consolation is usually severely limited. Caretakers are in constant danger of overprotecting others and exhausting themselves. They often take too much responsibility for others and too little for themselves. They give to others that which they are unable to accept. And by protecting too much and comforting too little, they deprive their charges of the opportunity to grow through trial and error.

Whether parents are overprotective or abusive, by inadequately comforting their successors, they cause the unnecessary and tragic chain of self-doubt to continue unbroken, and one disabled generation unconsciously deprives the next, and the next, unless something is done to reverse the process and to allow self-acceptance to become part of the heritage.

Childhood Questionnaire

The object of this questionnaire is to help you remember your feelings as a child. No scoring of answers is necessary. Careful consideration and response to each question—aloud to someone you trust or in writing to yourself—will help you to recall what you actually felt when the events occurred. The object is to sort out your feelings and to recreate your experience of childhood.

1. Do you remember feeling lonely often as a child?

2. Did you often keep your feelings, especially your bad feelings, to yourself?

3. Were you especially sensitive? Were your feelings hurt by things that didn't seem to hurt others as much? Were you able to sense when others were hurt even when they tried to hide it?

4. Was there at least one adult who respected your thoughts and feelings? Was there someone there who could get you to talk about your thoughts and feelings when you were hurting? Was there someone to comfort you when you were unhappy?

5. Did you feel overprotected, controlled or smothered? Were you frequently prevented from doing what you felt you could and should be allowed to do? Were there many rules in your home and punishments for breaking them?

6. Were you treated with respect? Were you encouraged to take risks and experiment? Were you praised when you were successful and comforted when you weren't?

7. Were you extremely obedient or extremely disobedient (a very good or very bad kid) much of the time?

8. Did you worry about whether you were good enough?

9. Did you have any physical handicap or learning disability which made you feel different from other children? Did you feel different for any reason (such as race, religion or economic class)?

10. Did you receive unconditional love—affection unrelated to your actions or accomplishments?

11. Did you feel a great deal was expected of you—perhaps more than you could live up to? Or was very little expected because it was assumed you would never accomplish much?

12. Were you criticized far more often than you were praised?

13. Did you have to devote a substantial amount of time to working in or outside the home?

14. Were you physically abused? Were you sexually abused?

15. Were you separated from one or both of your parents for a prolonged period prior to your eighteenth birthday?

16. Did you have a difficult time with a stepparent or guardian?

17. Did you spend any time at boarding school, foster home or other institution?

18. Were either of your parents or guardians psychologically ill? Did either of your parents or guardians abuse alcohol or drugs?

19. Were either of your parents emotionally or physically dependent on you prior to your eighteenth birthday?

20. Were you often afraid of one of your parents or guardians or siblings?

21. Did your parents argue frequently? Do you remember

being afraid and wanting, or even trying, to get them to stop?

22. Did you feel that your parent(s) always wanted the best for you even if he or she (they) didn't agree with you or were angry at you?

Sensitivity, loneliness, lack of comforting, overprotection, disrespect, neglect and pain are the things that predispose people to self-doubt and Mind Traps.

You may protest that your childhood pain was less severe than many others. You may point out that everyone's childhood has painful, lonely times and that most children don't get respect, understanding or comforting. I couldn't agree more. And that's exactly why self-doubt and Mind Traps are universal.

That other children suffered too, and perhaps even more, doesn't make *your* pain any less. You felt whatever you felt as a child and it affected you profoundly. It was the only life you knew and you had little or nothing with which to compare it. The child you were lives on in you now. Your childhood experiences continue to shape your current identity, and your identity controls your life.

To change you don't have to undertake a detailed exploration of your childhood. But you do need to change your attitudes about yourself as a child. Unless you begin to feel compassion for the hurt and lonely child in you, that child will continue to feel self-doubt, fear and other painful feelings like anger, resentment, guilt and humiliation. If you don't have compassion for yourself, you will continue to use Mind Traps to avoid having to face the troubled and uncomforted child within you.

CHAPTER 3

The Familiarity Principle

"[Moosbrugger] had the feeling that he was wearing the Moosbrugger of his life like an old coat; he opened it a little, now and again, and the most wondrous lining came gushing out in forest-green waves of silk."

Robert Musil,
from *The Man Without Qualities*

"As [we believe] we are, so we do; and as we do, so it is done to us; we are the builders of our fortunes."

Ralph Waldo Emerson

The Power of Our Familiar Identities

Identity determines destiny. Who you believe you are determines how you observe the world and affects everything you do. All your experiences and actions pass through the filter of your identity.

Stand back and consider yourself. Whether you are content with yourself or not, you are accustomed to being the way you are.

Familiarity is not just a matter of isolated habits but of your entire sense of yourself: how you are accustomed to acting, how you are accustomed to feeling about yourself, how you are accustomed to being treated. Behaving or being treated in ways that are inconsistent with your experience makes you feel awkward and artificial.

The Familiarity Principle:

It is uncomfortable to act or be treated in unfamiliar ways. People cannot tolerate acting or being treated as if they were someone different than they are used to and therefore believe themselves to be. Anyone who begins to behave or be treated in unfamiliar ways, will become increasingly uncomfortable.

Though we consciously prefer comfort to discomfort, the Familiarity Principle has far more influence over our actions than the pleasure principle. When given a choice, we are likely to choose pleasure over pain, unless we are unaccustomed to pleasure and accustomed to pain. (The phrase "comfort zone" is sometimes used to describe habits, actions and feelings which feel familiar. But "comfort zone" is a misnomer. We usually do what is familiar, not what is more comfortable or beneficial.)

If the people you know suddenly began treating you with greater respect, warmth and consideration than you are accustomed to, you might be surprised at first and delighted. But before long your delight would fade and be replaced by awkwardness, discomfort and disbelief. You might begin to wonder what in the world they were up to and who put them up to this charade. You would feel uncomfortable. You would be in crisis.

The Chinese word for "crisis" is an apt combination of

two characters: *danger* and *opportunity.* Unfortunately, when faced with the identity crisis essential to any significant personal change, many people are so intimidated by the danger that they miss the opportunity.

"Change," "learning," "growth" and "self-discovery" are all labels for a single process. This process requires acting and being seen as someone different than you have ever been. The old you must be encouraged to step down and allow the new you to take its place. If you want to change, you must be willing to endure the discomfort of an identity crisis.

You can accomplish self-initiated change only if you are willing to step off into the unknown and go through an identity crisis. The phrase "identity crisis" usually has a negative connotation, but the truth is these crises are essential for growth. Identity crises occur naturally in adolescence and in other normal transition times like mid-life.

To change you must be willing to act as if you are already the person you would respect more. You will feel artificial and anxious while you experiment with self-respect-generating actions. If you're willing to persist at feeling awkward but proud as you try to change, you'll be on the right track.

Our pasts place blinders around our eyes, making it easy to keep traveling in familiar ruts. People can become distressed by change even if they know that the change is for the better—like graduating from school, receiving a promotion or getting into shape.

People do whatever is necessary to get others to treat them as they are used to and believe they deserve—not too much better and not too much worse. As we move from malleable and impressionable childhood into adolescence and beyond, we live in an increasingly predictable familiarity zone of our own creation.

The successful but lonely and unfulfilled workaholic physician I referred to in the previous chapter tried many times to take better care of himself, to get involved in recreational activities, to treat his wife and others with greater respect and to stop bullying people with his explosive temper. But people's reactions to his new behavior made him feel strange. Some people acted unusually warm to him. Others were wary of his uncharacteristic attitude. To do well was inconsistent with his sense of himself and his worth. His new behavior made him feel like a good person. This exaggerated his sense of hypocrisy. Instead of enduring the period of discomfort necessary for change, his familiar identity would reassert itself and he would return to familiar lifelong habits.

New romantic love can cause a temporary suspension of the Familiarity Principle. A couple falls in love. They treat each other wonderfully at first. But once the intensity of their infatuation has dwindled, one partner may begin to protest in words or actions: "You've got to take me off this pedestal. I'm not as great as you think I am."

The Familiarity Principle can manifest itself in positive ways as well. There are some people whose childhoods accustomed them to feeling worthwhile, respected and respectful. Anything else feels wrong and they are unwilling to endure being treated badly. These are rare, fortunate people whose parents were respectful of their ability to learn from experience; parents who were considerate of their children's feelings. For better or for worse, people can only accept being treated in familiar ways.

Where Do Mind Traps Come In?

Mind Traps are habitual self-defeating attitudes. Each Mind Trap has one of two reassuring purposes. It tries to reassure you either about your worth or about your familiar sense of yourself. Mind Traps allow you to say to yourself, "I'm not worthless, but I'm not that great, either. I'm just who I've always believed I am." Mind Traps keep you scrambling up and sliding down the slope of self-doubt in continuous fear of falling into the feeling of worthlessness at one end and catapulting into the panic of an identity crisis at the other.

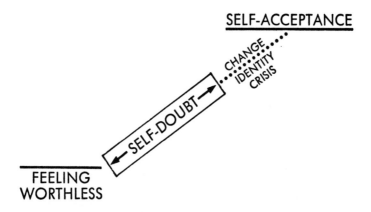

Mind Traps rob you of the chance to realize your potential in the present. Mind Traps keep you stuck in the past because they maintain your safe but sorry self-doubting identity. They prevent you from having compassion for your pain and from acting with self-respect. As a result, they make self-acceptance and well-being impossible.

CHAPTER 4

The Self-Doubt Trap

> "What we must decide is perhaps how we are valuable rather than how valuable we are."
>
> Edgar Z. Friedenberg

The Self-Doubt Trap:

"I have doubts about myself. I'm afraid there may be something wrong with me."

Commonly Associated Features

People in *The Self-Doubt Trap* may have some of the following characteristics:

- fear of not being good enough
- anxiety when things are going well
- difficulty accepting honest praise
- reluctance to take on new responsibilities or to try new things

- tendency to be jealous
- reluctance to expose true feelings
- inability to accept comforting except when in extreme pain
- need to impress others with their accomplishments or appearance
- tendency to be opinionated and defensive
- need to be in control and right, or at least not wrong
- tendency to place others' needs and wishes ahead of their own
- critical and blaming of themselves or others
- difficulty making decisions and dependency on the opinions of others
- tendency to be disrespectful or inconsiderate, especially to people most important to them
- addictions to harmful people, substances or habits
- tendency to avoid confrontations at almost any cost

Physician, Heal Thyself

Having used myself as an example to introduce the ideas of self-doubt and Mind Traps, I will complete the story by describing how I began to change from self-doubt to self-acceptance.

As I have already explained, at thirty-three I was a desperately unhappy man. This was true despite my success and despite the love and approval others offered me. Then, around the time of my agonizing self-examination depicted in Chapter One, I began to wake up. Two things helped to arouse me—my desperation and confrontations by two friends.

My friends individually took me aside. They both

expressed grave concern. They told me I looked terrible. One predicted I was about to have a heart attack. Although I was doing my best to hide my feelings about myself, apparently I looked as bad as I felt. It was humiliating to be a psychiatrist and a respected administrator yet be so miserable and out of control of my life.

With my friends' help I began to stand back from myself and be more objective and compassionate. If you want to change, this is the first and most critical step.

I was skilled at helping others to stand back from themselves, sort out their difficulties and learn to be compassionate towards themselves. Why not use that ability to help myself? Physician heal thyself . . . indeed!

I began to consider the following possibilities: What if the people who knew me well were right? They had seen me at my worst, when my shortcomings were exposed. Yet these people kept telling me I was special—that I was smart, loving, energetic, good with others, willing to take on the responsibility of influencing others' lives and blessed with a fine sense of humor, though you certainly couldn't confirm that with my family at the time! What if I were to accept that I, like everyone else, had strengths and weaknesses? What if there was and had never been anything wrong with me? What if my feelings of inadequacy were merely confusion, hurt and fear inside me—a scummy residue of loneliness and pain from childhood? What if I were to seriously consider my friends' contentions that I did have special gifts?

These prospects should have reassured me. Yet I felt more anxious than relieved. There I was weighing the possibility that I might have more going for me than I had ever believed. Instead of being delighted, I was uncomfortable. Why didn't the possibility that I need no longer worry about my intrinsic worth reassure me? Being afraid that there was nothing wrong with me provided the clue that helped me change my attitude and beliefs about myself.

Slowly my anxiety became understandable. If I really had my share of strengths, what was I supposed to do with them? I had spent years focusing my energy on trying to prove the unprovable—that I wasn't defective. If I were to stop worrying about my deficiencies and start considering that I had something to offer, the entire focus of my life would shift from trying to *prove* myself worthy, to trying to *use* myself well.

These positive considerations frightened me. They undermined my lifelong sense of myself. If these new possibilities were true, then I was not who I had always believed myself to be. I was not intrinsically inadequate and flawed, someone who had to hide certain aspects of himself. I had to start thinking of myself as someone blessed with talents to be discovered, refined and used.

This was a revolutionary concept: *Perhaps there had never been anything wrong with me except my belief that there was something wrong.* I had to suspend my self-doubt and consider the possibility that my sense of defectiveness was a mistaken belief from childhood, a mistaken belief that became a core part of my habitual sense of myself.

If I were ever to acquire a new identity, I would have to be willing to become someone I had never known, a new person, a stranger. It would mean leaving the predictability of my familiar self-doubting identity. It involved trying-on-for-size a new self-concept: Whoever I could and might become, I was already good enough to stop worrying about my worth. I could accept myself without further accomplishments or approval from others.

This leap of faith in my worth would be a positive identity crisis. But going through an identity crisis was only half the challenge. Escaping from self-doubt also meant accepting the responsibility for choosing how to best use myself and my time. It meant keeping track of how I was doing by learning how to read my thoughts and feelings instead of looking primarily to others' reactions for guidance.

This new identity would mean self-respect and satisfaction would be entirely up to me to arrange, instead of something I had a right to expect from someone else. *If I wanted self-respect, I had to act in ways I respected.* And I'd have to be willing to take whatever steps were necessary to make certain I was treated with respect.

Changing would mean not being in control. It would mean leaving my secure but disturbing nest of habits and feelings about myself and stepping off into the unknown. It would mean trying to fly as best I could, instead of waiting until I proved to myself that my wings would guarantee me safe flight.

Once I seriously considered this new attitude, I had no choice. I realized I had been running all my life from fear of growing up and accepting responsibility for myself. I had been hiding these fears behind my fear of not being good enough. I had been exhausting myself in futile efforts to prove my worth. But the irony was no one except myself was asking for any proof of my worth. My self-doubt was entirely my issue.

I began to realize there was no use wasting any more time worrying about whether I was good enough. My wings would develop only if they were used. How well they would carry me was limited only by my genetic gifts and my willingness to try. My desperation helped get me going. Desperation can be a great thing if you use it well. It can free you up, blast you out of ruts. Being forced to reevaluate old beliefs can clear new paths by stimulating your creativity.

I began to reassess my priorities. I gave up being an administrator, cut back on my hours as a therapist and reduced my financial commitments and expectations. I started to write more, to take better care of myself and to pay more attention to my family.

I haven't felt serious concern about my worth in a decade. Self-respect has become my highest priority. That is, my self-respect takes precedence over my ambitions. As a result and not surprisingly, my self-respect has increased. And my marriage, family life and health have improved along with it. I'm doing the best I can—that's all I can do. I can't control results and I have even less say about whether or not my efforts will be rewarded.

I admit, I'm still often anxious. But I'm actually proud to have my share of disappointments and failures because they are evidence of my willingness to take risks in order to discover what I have to offer. At least now I can enjoy tenderness, comforting and occasional moments of intimacy and fulfillment.

I believe this is about as good as life gets.

Escape Route
Exposing the Trap

The Self-Doubt Trap is the crucial Mind Trap, the moving force behind all the others. Most people suffer from it to some degree. Other Mind Traps develop during childhood and adolescence to defend again this most fundamental of Mind Traps—self-doubt based on fear of defectiveness.

It is critical to get off this train of thought. *The Self-Doubt Trap* takes you in circles and gets you nowhere except more and more lost in your habitual self-doubting identity. I urge you to use your unique human capacity for self-observation. Please stand back from yourself and consider this argument:

No one but you is measuring your worth as a human being. No one but you believes that there may be something inherently and perhaps irreversibly wrong with you. (If someone questions your value, doesn't that reflect his or her own self-doubt rather than anything about your human essence?)

No one has the right to decide any person's worth, including one's own. People must not be regarded as objects to be weighed, measured, categorized and allocated. Materialism must not be allowed to contaminate our attitudes towards ourselves.

There is no such thing as a defective person! Is a baby born mentally retarded or without arms of less value than one who is physically normal? Any standard of measurement must be arbitrarily based on someone's biased value system and is therefore debatable.

A person's intrinsic worth is a indefinable concept at best. At worst, *the idea of an individual's or a group's relative worth is the most destructive of human ideas.* It alienates people from one another. It alienates you from yourself.

Of the millions of sperm racing to fertilize your mother's ovum, yours made it. You became a conscious human being. That's a miracle of considerable magnitude. That miracle—your existence—has value. And that's the only intrinsic value you ever need worry about. *To be alive is to have worth.* The question of whether any one is good "enough" becomes insanely trivial when compared to the wonder of existing at all. *The Self-Doubt Trap* takes you on a detour from facing the most challenging question of your life—an immensely more important, relevant and answerable question than that of personal worth: *"What's the most self-respecting and meaningful use of my time?"*

What makes this question difficult is that you must answer it for yourself. No one else can give you the "right" answer. The responsibility implied by this question is frightening. The more trapped you are in self-doubt, the more afraid you will be to search for your answer. Stuck in self-doubt, you will wonder: "Who am I to decide the best use of what I have within me? How can I rely on myself to make good decisions?"

Mind Traps are attempts to avoid facing life's difficult

issues. Everyone must find meaning, make choices, deal with loneliness and face losses. Instead of facing these frightening dilemmas, people with self-doubt find it easier to obey someone else's prescriptions and rules for life, to pursue power, money, prestige and even vengeance, to try controlling other people's lives, to focus their attention on doubts about whether they are made of the right stuff or to worry about whether they deserve to be alive at all. These are all enervating, demeaning and debilitating distractions.

The path of least resistance is to be either obedient or disobedient to the expectations of others. To try to figure out what *you* believe is right is a far greater burden. Blinded by preoccupation with success, failure and the opinions of others or numbed by substance abuse, people with self-doubt unconsciously try to sidestep humanity's unavoidable enigmas for which no one has certain answers.

Being plagued by questions like: "What's wrong with me?" and "How can I prove myself?" is disturbing. Yet it is easier than accepting your worth, because accepting one's worth leads to more difficult and responsible questions, such as "What's the point of my life? Why am I here? What am I supposed to do with myself for the rest of my time?"

To make substantial and lasting changes, you must give up your self-doubt and other Mind Traps and take responsibility for your own well-being. Taking this step would make you a rare person indeed.

Why do so many people avoid changing and accepting full responsibility for themselves? Because of fear. Self-doubt and the other Mind Traps are based on three kinds of fear. The first is *fear of worthlessness.* This originates in childhood misunderstanding, as discussed in Chapter 2. The second is *fear of loss of your habitual identity,* as discussed in Chapter 3. The third is *fear of life's uncertainties.*

Why is it so hard to face these fears? Because most people are brought up in a conventional family culture. In such a culture, more emphasis is placed on conformity to adult expectations about appearances and external results than on compassionate understanding of feelings and respect for oneself and others. "Be a good child and everything will be okay," one is told—as if obedience to rules and human authority is the most important issue in life. Both "good" and "bad" children grow up with self-doubt. The "bad" ones have been made to feel defective. The "good" ones feel like hypocrites. They know how much acting they've had to do to gain approval.

Whether children's self-doubts come primarily from their experiences with well-intentioned but overprotective parents or from circumstances of severe poverty, abuse and discrimination, the effects are similar. Most children never learn the value of making compassion and self-respect the most important issues in life.

Self-worth and self-respect are worlds apart. Self-worth is a birthright and must be accepted on faith. It's beyond proof. Self-worth is included in the package, provided by the manufacturer. Anyone concerned about your inherent worth should feel free to contact that manufacturer.

The same is not true of self-respect. *Self-respect is your personal responsibility and opportunity.* It is the most satisfying of feelings. It can only be earned by honest, wholehearted efforts directed toward a goal that *feels* right and true to you.

Self-respect often requires overcoming fear of possible consequences, like standing up to a fearsome authority for what you believe is right. Pushing yourself to overcome obstacles for what *you* believe in is necessary if you want to earn self-respect. And the greater the fears that must be encountered, the greater the feeling of self-respect earned.

Self-respect is based on actions true to your inborn sense of what is right, not conformity to others' expectations. Self-respect requires you to try to do your best at something that seems worthwhile to *you.* If you keep doing that, self-respect is guaranteed.

You'll never reach your potential as long as you try to prove your worth. As long as you remain preoccupied with your worth or lack of worth, you'll be obsessed with results and waste your time trying to look good to others. As a result, you won't experiment enough. You'll be afraid to feel and look awkward. This will prevent you from discovering your hidden talents, especially those which would require you to threaten another person's comfort and control. If you exhaust yourself trying to hide your defects and prove your worth, *you won't use yourself well.* And you'll live with a nagging sense of dissatisfaction no matter how successful you are. (For more on proving your worth, see Part 8, *Prove Your Worth Traps.*)

To get the most from life, you also must come to terms with your mortality. But here again self-doubt gets in your way. Self-doubt makes the idea of death work against you rather than for you. As long as you worry about your worth, you'll be afraid to look squarely at death and face the possibility that you may die at any moment. To die before you believe you've proven your worth would make you feel your entire life had been worthless. For this reason anything that reminds you of death, such as the death of someone close to you, getting ill, or reaching the age at which a loved one died, will increase your desperation to prove your worth as soon as possible. Your unconscious, silent and futile plea is: "I can't die yet—I haven't even begun to earn my right to be here."

People avoid facing their mortality in all kinds of ways. Examples are men who get divorced and remarry someone younger so they don't have to be reminded of their own aging, or women who endure repeated plastic surgeries to eliminate evidence of the passage of time. Some people are so afraid of death, they decide to escape the threat of it constantly hanging over their dissatisfied heads and rush to get it over with.

Unfortunately, self-worth must be accepted on faith. It

cannot be earned or proven. And self-doubt makes it impossible to accept your worth, no matter what you do. Your habitual self-doubting identity traps you.

However, if you are willing to take the steps necessary to gain self-acceptance, if you can accept your inner worth as a given, you'll be able to use your sense of limited time to inspire you to make the most of yourself and the time you have left. Once concern about self-worth is set aside, awareness of your mortality can help make each moment more valuable.

A New Direction

Try adopting the following attitude:

I didn't ask to be here, but here I am anyway. And I'm not going to be here forever. I've been given inherited talents and weaknesses. I had no say about my genetic capacities. I'm a product of my past—my inheritance and my experiences. I can't change that. However, I *do* have some say about how I act now.

I am not who I was years ago, I am not who I may be sometime in the future, and I may not be who others want me to be. I'm not even who I have believed I am. Like it or not, *I am exactly who I am.* And I'd like to find out who that is and who I could grow to become.

I do have some choices and because I do, I can choose to take risks and experiment to find out what I'm capable of. I can try on different attitudes that seem to offer more than my familiar attitudes. I can behave differently, in new ways that seem preferable to my habits.

I will concentrate on developing my strengths, instead of trying to hide or compensate for my weaknesses. The only way I can discover what I have to offer is by exploring various activities. It's up to me to locate my wellsprings of talent. I can experiment until I find those pursuits that make me feel better about myself and come to me more readily than other activities.

And since I have control over *how* I do whatever I'm doing, why not do the best I can? Maybe what I do and what I accomplish is less important than *how* I do it. Perhaps it is less important to do the right things than to do things for the right reasons. If I do things for the right reasons, I'll earn self-respect automatically. And the more difficult the thing I try to accomplish, the more self-respect I'll earn.

If I'm fortunate enough to succeed at something I feel good about, then not only will I earn self-respect, I'll also feel fulfilled. If I fail despite my best efforts, I'll still have self-respect.

So the question: "Do you have value as a person?" turns out to be foolish and destructive. You are a person. Therefore you have value. Find out what you have to offer, refine your abilities and get satisfaction from using your talents in ways that earn self-respect. If you manage that, you will keep learning, growing and changing.

PART 2

The Importance of Feelings

There is much confusion and a great deal of sloppy thinking about feelings. Misconceptions range from the prescription "go with your feelings," to the idea that feelings are less important than rational thinking.

Feelings get special emphasis in this book because they play two crucial roles in human experience. Feelings are the reason anyone cares about anything in life. Without feelings, life would have no quality, good or bad. Feelings contribute the color, music and texture to all other aspects of being.

Another pivotal role of feelings is their important message value. The better you become at understanding what your feelings are saying to you, the better you can manage your life. Learning to decipher feelings' messages is necessary if you hope to satisfy your needs. The messages provided by your feelings let you know what is right and wrong for you in any given situation. Feelings, interpreted as signals, are the best guide to personal ethics.

Before exploring the meaning of specific feelings, we must first consider the concept of the human spirit.

CHAPTER 5

Feelings and the Human Spirit

Before we can discuss how to handle feelings, we must address a controversial concept—the human spirit. There can be no practical, in-depth understanding of feelings until you come to grips with the idea of the human spirit.

- Where do feelings come from?

- What causes me to feel close to other people?

- What makes me want companionship?

- What is the source of my needs, intuition and creativity?

- How can I use my feelings?

It is impossible to answer these questions or make sense of human experiences in which feelings are involved without the concept of the human spirit. The idea of the human spirit is pivotal to achieving personal understanding and self-change.

If you reject the human spirit because you consider it an irrational and unscientific concept, you may find this chapter valuable. In this chapter the term "human spirit" is defined in a restricted sense, without religious connotations.

The Spirit Defined

Every person is born with a human spirit. The spirit, as I am defining it, is that which makes each individual unique. The human spirit is the wellspring of energy for the mind and body. It is the source of each person's talents, sensitivities, vulnerabilities, hopes, needs, desires, inspiration, creativity and feelings. People's spirits are made up of various mixtures of all these ingredients.

Studies have demonstrated that genes significantly influence lifelong individual traits.[1] Each person's spiritual endowment is unique. But every person has enough in common with others to enable one person to understand another, to sympathize with another, to love another and, if that person has been abused and hurt enough, to hate another. The spirit is the connection between mind and body, between one person and another, between each person and the rest of the cosmos.

Personality and the Human Spirit

Personality and human spirit are concepts that should not be confused. The term "personality" refers to a person's habitual style of dealing with life. It includes a person's characteristic ways of thinking, speaking and acting. Personality also includes a person's particular set of Mind Traps.

A person's personality is the way that person deals with the world. The spirit provides the necessary resources. Personality includes habitual attitudes and behavior. A person's personality develops from experience. Spirits are inborn.

Evidence For the Human Spirit

Let's consider the kind of evidence we have for this abstract idea of a human spirit—the source of feelings and

[1]Thomas, A., and Chess, S. Temperament and Development. *Brunner/Mazel: New York, 1977.*

the invisible link between people.

A couple had been married for forty years. After his wife died, the widowed husband became lonely and depressed and began having difficulty with his heart. Within two months, despite counseling and medical treatment, he, too, passed away. Scientists may come up with better and better explanations of what went wrong in the man's body to cause him to die so suddenly. But they will never find a better explanation of *why* he died than that his spirit lost its will to live on this earth without his lifelong companion.

Astronomers accept the existence of "black holes," areas in space thought to be due to stars so dense that even light waves can't escape from them. Although intangible and not directly measurable, the existence of black holes was accepted because it was the best available explanation for otherwise inexplicable manifestations in space. Yet there is at least as much data close at hand for the intangible, easily wounded, but irrepressible and creative human spirit.

Recall some of the manifestations of the human spirit as I have defined it: energy, needs, will, creativity and feelings. Notice that all these are features of ourselves which we can identify by looking within ourselves. They are *subjective,* experiential phenomena. There will never be direct *objective* proof of the human spirit. Just as with black holes, we can only indirectly establish the spirit's existence and nature.

The immaterial, magical quality of closeness between people is found in other experiences, but none more commonly or clearly than in the varieties of love: What is the source of the connection between people in love? Could the mind alone be the source of love? Surely we can be of like mind and yet not feel love for one another. Imagine a group of bankers concurring with the reasoning of a colleague. Do they love him just because they are in agreement?

If not primarily mental, could love be mostly a bodily function? People who have sex often aren't in love with each other. Conversely, people may be deeply in love and still yearn for their first touch. And many people love their children and friends deeply without any sexual desire.

So both mind and body participate in love, but they are not its essence. To speak of any love without an emotional and spiritual connection implied makes the word "love" meaningless. Love in any of its myriad forms is a manifestation of the spirit. No other concept will do.

Love is only one example of the human spirit in action. There are many other ways in which people's spirits make contact. People who join together to help victims of accidents sense the linking of their spirits as a positive feeling of comradery. Upon seeing another person in need, their immediate, spontaneous reaction was to band together to help. (Perhaps people in large cities who ignore a person screaming for help are evidence of the poisoning and suffocation of the human spirit in overcrowded conditions.)

The writer and naturalist Anne Dillard in her book *Teaching a Stone To Talk*[2] describes her thoughts and feelings after viewing a total eclipse of the sun:

> Seeing this black body was like seeing a mushroom cloud . . . In the deeps are the violence and terror of which psychology has warned us. But if you ride these monsters deeper down, if you drop with them farther over the world's rim, you find that our sciences cannot locate or name, the substrate, the ocean or matrix or ether which buoys the rest, which gives goodness its power for good, and evil its power for evil, the unified field: our complex and inexplicable caring for each other and for our life together here. This is given. It is not learned.

This inborn, unlearned caring Dillard mentions is felt strongly after witnessing a phenomenon which gives the

[2]Anne Dillard, *Teaching a Stone to Talk*, (New York: Harper and Row, 1982).

sense of intense shared emotion. Anne Dillard experienced this after observing a dramatic eclipse. Others may feel that closeness spending the night with a stranger in a foxhole under an artillery barrage, or even waiting in an elevator stuck between floors.

You can sense the individual spirit in others by looking deeply into their eyes. A way of recognizing the human spirit in yourself is to note the different feelings you get around different people. Around some people you may feel uncomfortable and defensive even if they have not attacked or offended you in any way. In the presence of other people you may feel safe and encouraged, even though it is the first time you've met them and even before there has been any interchange between you. It is a combination of your mind, body and spirit which reacts in different ways to different people and causes you to feel differently about each of them.

Psychology, Psychiatry and the Human Spirit

Unfortunately, modern psychology and psychiatry miss the advantages of recognizing and incorporating the human spirit in their theories.[3] These fields denigrate feelings, subordinating them to the intellect and to rational thinking.

Feelings and rational thought continue to be seen as diametrically opposed phenomena, like bad and good, night and day. But memory requires the harmonious coordination of rational thinking and feelings. A subtle interplay of feeling and intellect is also necessary for the intuitive hunches and spontaneous insights essential to creativity in any field.

In their preoccupation with being scientific, psychologists

---

[3]*The closest thing to the concept of the human spirit to be found in modern psychology/psychiatry is the concept of the "true self" as used by a certain group of psychoanalysts (including Winnecott and A. Miller). I will use the terms "spirit" and "true self" interchangeably to denote the intangible part of a person that is the repository of one's inborn and unique nature. This true self should be distinguished from the "false self" or "habitual self" contaminated with self-doubt and Mind Traps.*

have given up the human spirit (and its primary language, feelings) as the concept unifying mind and body, preferring to study only those aspects of our beings and consciousness which are amenable to objective research or computer simulation. As a result, psychology and psychiatry lack a unifying spiritual element to help individuals lead ethical lives.

It shouldn't be surprising that psychology and psychiatry have been coopted by the same materialism that dominates our culture. Feelings are difficult to fit into a computer model of the mind. The spirit is nonmaterial and therefore cannot be studied directly. Objective proof of the existence of a human spirit is impossible. So scientists ignore the spirit and regard feelings as secondary phenomena.

The rejection of the human spirit as a necessary and practical concept in psychology persists despite the obvious importance of feelings in memory, despite the dominance of emotions over rational thought during childhood and during the most intense and meaningful moments in life, despite every great artist's explicit recognition of the importance of inspiration in their creations and despite the powerfully moving effects creative works have on those of us who witness them.

Feelings and the Human Spirit

Your feelings and sensations can provide you with a continuous stream of information about the moment-to-moment condition of your human spirit, of the child within you. Each person's human spirit sends messages in the form of feelings and bodily sensations (such as muscle tension, digestive problems, headaches, blushing of the cheeks, quickening of the heart or genital excitation). Attempts to shut out these messages are hazardous to your mind, body and spirit. You cannot betray your spirit without paying the price. The punishment for failing to nurture the human spirit with compassionate and self-respecting actions is to suffer from emptiness, dissatisfaction, bad feelings and ultimately physical deterioration.

Practical Applications

The idea of the human spirit has been extremely helpful to me in my personal life and in my work with others in two major ways. The first is the issue of feelings. Without the concept of the spirit, feelings are merely experiences—good and bad—that affect your life and at times interfere with rational thinking and action. But if you acknowledge the spirit, feelings can be recognized as its messages. Then feelings become an invaluable data source you can learn to use to guide your life in the direction of self-acceptance, self-respect and well-being.

Appreciating the human spirit can also help people take loving care of themselves for the first time. When I would encourage my clients to take better care of themselves before I began to use the concept of spirit, my advice almost invariably fell on deaf ears. Now even the most self-doubting of people will often begin to look after themselves better once they start to conceive of a needy, vulnerable and hurting spirit within them that needs their help.

You can blend these two practical advantages into a healthy attitude and way of life: "I am responsible for my own well-being. My feelings tell me how my spirit is doing and can help me decide how to nurture and enrich it."

Ethical Behavior and the Human Spirit

The human spirit thrives on compassion and respect; it withers without it. The well-being of our spirits requires that we treat others with warmth and consideration. It feels wrong to act maliciously, just as it feels wrong to be treated badly. You may be accustomed to acting or being treated badly—it may feel familiar, but it still feels bad.

"Treating others as you wish to be treated" is nothing but the Golden Rule, restated as a spiritual principle worth applying in one's daily life, rather than a religious rule which "should" be obeyed. The ability to recognize immediate ill-effects on yourself and your spirit can help you guide your actions in healthy directions more effectively than fear of punishment at some later time. And by acting in concert with an inner sense of right you'll enjoy the wonderful experience of increasing your self-respect instead of merely feeling you have been obedient.

In *Anna Karenina,* Tolstoy gives valuable insight into the potential of the human spirit. Levin, a fair and thoughtful man, is tortured by self-doubt and concerns about the right way to live. At the end of the novel, he turns his attention inward and discovers his spirit. This revelation transforms his sense of himself and his life:

> When he did not think, but just lived, he never ceased to be aware of the presence in his soul of an infallible judge who decided which of two possible courses of action was the better and which the worse, and instantly let him know if he did what he should not.

The "infallible judge" is a subtle inner feeling you may feel in your bones, your gut or your heart. If you aren't accustomed to feeling it, at first you must search for it. It will pass unnoticed unless carefully attended to. But, with time and practice, it will become more obvious and helpful.[4]

In order to lead an ethical and healthy life, you must listen to your inner sense of what is right and wrong, what gives you self-respect and what diminishes it.

---

[4]*The voice from your spirit can become as awesome as God's voice from the whirlwind to contrite and trembling Job. The human race has often shortchanged itself by ignoring and misinterpreting inner voices. Through the ages the tangible and objective have been much easier to visualize and believe in than anything internal and subjective. Most religions have capitulated to the materialism and have encouraged obedience to dogma instead of inner truth.*

PART 3

The Feelings Traps

CHAPTER 6

The "Bad Feelings Are Wrong" Trap

> "Pain and death are part of life. To reject them is to reject life itself."
>
> Havelock Ellis

> "There's nothing either good or bad, but thinking makes it so."
>
> William Shakespeare

The "Bad Feelings Are Wrong" Trap:

"When I'm unhappy, it's difficult to feel good about myself. Uncomfortable feelings (like anger, hurt, resentment and embarrassment) make me wonder what's wrong with me."

Commonly Associated Features

People in *The "Bad Feeling Are Wrong" Trap* may have the following characteristics:

- easily hurt by criticism

- unusual sensitivity to other people's feelings
- tendency to place others' needs and wishes ahead of their own
- reluctance to expose true feelings
- pessimism and self-blame
- difficulty accepting comforting except when they are in extreme pain
- anxiety when thing are going well
- difficulty accepting honest praise
- addictions to harmful people, substances or habits

The Seeker

Alex, age thirty, consulted me after reading my previous book. He was tall, handsome and talkative. Alex complained of intractable headaches. He had consulted numerous medical specialists over the years but all tests for physical causes were negative. He said he was turning to me in desperation. Alex hoped I could prescribe a psychiatric drug that would give him relief.

I told Alex that he had made a poor choice in selecting me as the latest prospect in his quest for the magic drug cure. Because I rarely see people who I believe would benefit from medications, I rarely prescribe them. I explained I would be delighted to work with him but would not give him drugs because I knew of none that would go to the root of his pain.

It would have been potentially hazardous to his mental and physical well-being to try to eliminate his headaches with tranquilizers and pain-killing drugs. Both these types of medication are addictive. And the more successful these drugs were at numbing his pain, the more they would insulate him from crucial information about himself, information he needed in order to achieve well-being.

I believed Alex's headaches could never be eradicated entirely—with or without drugs. But my experience convinced me that his headaches could be reduced in frequency and duration once he understood what precipitated them and changed his attitude about the meaning of his pain. I told Alex I could help him decipher messages in his pain that could help him arrange a more satisfying life. However, if he was determined to find someone who would give him drugs to eradicate his pain, I would be willing to refer him to expert psychiatrists who rely on psychoactive medications as their primary means of treatment.

Alex, an extremely intelligent and perceptive man, didn't know whether to laugh, cry, walk out or hit me. Instead, he agreed to go home, listen to the tape recording of our session and consider my offer. Since all the medicines he had taken previously had made him feel drugged without significant relief, he decided to give my approach a try.

After several abortive attempts at changing, Alex finally became desperate enough to begin a compassionate exploration of the meaning of his headaches. It became clear that for Alex, to be in pain was to be defective; to be pain-free would mean being whole, redeemed and worthwhile. Ultimately he realized that he had been looking for an expert to come up with the wonder drug that would eliminate his pain and thereby transform him into a worthwhile person.

Like so many others, Alex believed his salvation had to come from something *outside* himself. Because of his sense of inner darkness, his feeling of being flawed, he could not conceive of redemption resulting from a change in his *own* attitudes and behavior.

Alex's fear of being defective reflected itself in his fear of dying from the elusive pathology that was causing his headaches. It was as if behind his fear of illness and death was his wish for a physical cause, no matter how deadly.[1] Alex's fear of impending doom persisted despite having had headaches for more than a decade without evidence of any physical cause.

Self-doubt and other Mind Traps dull intelligence. They rob you of your ability to be rational about yourself. No matter how smart you may be about anything else, self-doubt causes you to be stupid about yourself.

Alex eventually became desperate. He felt trapped between fear of dying and his wish to escape discomfort, if not by drugs, then by suicide if necessary. I pointed out the irony of his situation. He was saying in effect, "I'm afraid I'm dying from whatever is causing this pain, and if it doesn't stop, I'll kill myself." It's like ordering the man holding a gun to his head to drop it or you'll kill him, or drinking yourself to death to avoid your fear of death.

At the time of our initial visit, Alex earned a living as a draftsman. Although he admitted that drafting had always bored him, Alex's work had always delighted his employers. He had the competence of an architect without the formal education. But because of his headaches, Alex frequently had to quit working. The truth was he hated working with lifeless drawings in sterile offices.

By standing back from himself and reviewing his life out loud, Alex began to realize how sensitive he was to everything and everyone around him. When others were upset Alex felt their pain even if they tried to hide it. He felt lonely and meaningless. Alex couldn't sustain a commitment to a job or a close relationship with a woman and he felt inadequate as a result.

---

[1] *F. Kafka and L. Wittgenstein both wrote that they felt strange emotional relief once their fatal illnesses were diagnosed. They felt as if the source of their lifelong inner turmoil and feeling of defectiveness had finally become manifest and was no longer a hidden enemy lurking inside them. It is not rare for brilliant people to believe that they will die young, especially those who have had painful, emotionally deprived childhoods.*

Because of his fears of worthlessness, at first Alex was terrified to look closely at the meaning of his physical and emotional pain. Alex believed his bad feelings were evidence of his defectiveness. Fortunately he decided to become courageous. *Courage is the willingness to confront and overcome pain and fear in order to do what you sense is right.*

Alex began to use his discomfort to guide his actions. He recognized that his vulnerable spirit was so intolerant and demanding that he had to pay close attention to its cries for help. To ignore his spirit for any length of time meant suffering from extreme headaches. He really had no choice once he understood what his feelings meant. He began to devote himself to doing what he sensed his spirit required instead of trying to accommodate his life to conventional expectations. He began to appreciate that his was a strange but wonderfully unique spirit and he simply had to work with it and not against it. Trying to please others had never worked for him anyway.

Eventually, by listening to his feelings and by engaging in trial and error experiments with various careers, Alex made the decision to become a landscape architect. Since then, he has earned a degree in the field and married.

Although Alex is still subject to headaches from time to time, he can almost invariably identify their source by compassionately examining himself and his life. Sometimes his headaches are precipitated by emotional stress, sometimes by insufficient rest or recreation and sometimes by just the need to be out in nature. By changing how he is handling some aspect of his life, he can avoid getting headaches or at least obtain some relief; for example, by cutting down on his work hours or by going for a long hike in the wilderness.

Alex now appreciates that whatever the external cost, the needs of his spirit must come first if he is to have any hope of well-being. He is one of those people who are both gifted and burdened by an eccentric and demanding spirit—a spirit that must be continuously monitored and regularly indulged.

Escape Route
Exposing the Trap

The *"Bad Feelings Are Wrong"* Trap is a common and serious misunderstanding about the uncomfortable feelings that are part of life. It is the confusion of *feeling bad* with *being bad.*

To achieve well-being it is imperative to eliminate the fallacy that bad feelings are wrong. Bad feelings are neither "right" nor "wrong." They *are* uncomfortable. Bad feelings are messages to be understood so you can try to remedy them or at least arrange for comforting from others.

Because there is no such thing as a defective person, bad feelings do not reflect defectiveness. In Chapter Two, we examined the origins of self-doubt in childhood pain. Children who are not adequately respected, encouraged and comforted grow up to be self-doubting adults who don't respect themselves and don't seek out or accept comforting for their emotional pain—pain often consciously experienced only as anger, shame, resentment and blame; pain numbed by overwork, alcohol, food and drugs.

People with self-doubt confuse discomfort with defectiveness. The more they doubt their worth, the more discomfort makes sense to them. It fits their sense of themselves to be unhappy. Their pain is a familiar ache, a reminder and confirmation of their worst fears, that they are not what they should be in some way. Bad feelings reinforce their fears. *The Self-Doubt Trap* and *The "Bad Feelings Are Wrong" Trap* thus work together to keep people stuck in self-doubt.

Abused children always feel as if they are somehow bad and deserve the punishment they receive. The same inappropriate and demoralizing guilt occurs with the majority of rape victims. Self-doubt makes people easy prey to *The "Bad Feelings Are Wrong" Trap*—when treated badly they feel wrong and bad, even if they are innocent victims.

The antidote is self-acceptance and a reinterpretation of the meaning of feelings. Feelings are signals. A disturbing feeling is a cry from the vulnerable and needy child within. To blame yourself for your bad feelings is cruel. To criticize yourself for feeling unhappy is to waste the opportunity to use feelings as data to help guide your decisions.

Do you doubt yourself and your worth more when you're dissatisfied and unhappy? Reflect on the last time you felt hurt, angry or embarrassed. Although it may be disagreeable, carefully recall the incident—it was probably some kind of loss, rejection or failure. Did you feel bad about yourself at the time? Keeping the uncomfortable incident in mind, stand back from yourself in your mind's eye and imagine that a defenseless vulnerable child in you was upset by the incident. Wouldn't any vulnerable child have been hurt, angered or frightened by what happened?

Feeling bad means your spirit is hurting and that something may be wrong with the way you are living your life. Feeling bad doesn't mean that there is something wrong with *you.* Even guilt and resentment can be looked upon as spiritual experiences. Grief about the death of a friend speaks for the spirit as eloquently as being moved to tears by the miracle of birth or a magnificent sunrise. Feelings, good or bad, say nothing about your intrinsic value. Uncomfortable feelings needn't release a deluge of self-doubt, self-condemnation and self-pity. Bad feelings are an opportunity for compassion and comforting.

When you feel bad, you should carefully review each aspect of your current life and how you are managing it to discover the source of your spirit's unhappiness. Once you identify which aspect of your life is troubling you, you need to explore ways to change—for your own sake and for those around you.

A New Direction

Accept the fact that your feelings are never wrong. Messages from the human spirit speak in a code which you must learn to decipher, not to judge as right or wrong. To judge feelings *always* gets in the way of understanding feelings, and makes a good relationship with yourself or with anyone else impossible. Judging prevents you from using your feelings as guides.

Even if you feel hatred and think horrible thoughts about someone, that simply indicates how hurt and angry you must be. Terrible thoughts and feelings don't have to lead to terrible actions. *You are not responsible for your feelings. But you are responsible for your actions.*

Unless you pay attention to your feelings, try to understand them and then use that understanding to help take care of your spirit, you will end up destroying your spirit along with your mind and body.

The wife of one of my clients confessed to having had an affair. She knew of his numerous sexual infidelities during the past few years and said she was just trying to "balance the books." Yet, when he found out about her extramarital excursions, he fantasized breaking her legs and shooting one of the men he suspected.

Instead of acting on his impulses or blaming himself for having them, he chose to search for the meaning of his fantasies. He realized he felt profoundly wounded and threatened by her infidelity and appreciated how irrational and unfair his feelings were, given his own flagrant indiscretions. It helped him to recognize how the emotional neglect he experienced as a child may have sensitized him to the pain and humiliation of feeling like a cuckold.

By going to the heart of the issue, the hurt behind his anger and resentment, we were able to come up with better alternatives, alternatives more likely to heal his spirit than assaulting his wife and her lovers. He could stop blaming his wife and instead explain his pain. Then he could ask her to comfort and reassure him during his waves of grief and anger about her affairs. In return, he would be more consid-erate and loving towards her.

I warned him that these new ways of acting would be unfamiliar for both of them and would feel awkward and frightening. After all, neither of them had grown up in a loving family atmosphere and neither had experienced inti-macy with anyone other than a lover.

Fortunately, his wife was willing to cooperate in working at and adopting these new attitudes. Still, it will be a long time before they can begin to trust one another, since trust is foreign to both of them.

To find your way out of *The "Bad Feelings Are Wrong" Trap*, adopt the following attitudes:

If I hope to be loved and loving, to discover and develop my talents and to find meaningful ways to use my time, I must stay attuned to my spirit and allow it to guide me in my decisions. That means paying close attention to my feelings, because they are the medium through which my spirit is revealed to me.

I'm going to stop seeing myself as defective when I feel bad. Instead, I'm going to try to figure out why my spirit is in pain. Keeping a notebook and writing down what I'm feeling when I have strong feelings can help me learn to understand what my feelings are tell-ing me.

CHAPTER 7

The "Feelings Are Foolish" Trap

> "Reason guides but a small part of man and that the least interesting."
>
> Joseph Roux

The "Feelings Are Foolish" Trap:

"Strong feelings are uncomfortable and unreasonable. It's unfortunate to have them, worse to show them and useless to discuss them. To stay in control of my life, I need to control my feelings."

Commonly Associated Features

People in *The "Feelings Are Foolish" Trap* may have the following characteristics:

- sometimes coldly confrontational

- tendency to appear aloof or conceited

- easily upset by criticism and rejection but often won't admit it

- seldom tender, warm or sad

- tendency to be organized, punctual and rarely spontaneous

- reluctance to form close friendships

- difficulty accepting or offering comforting

- opinionated and defensive

- need to be in control and right, or at least not wrong

- only strong feelings are anger, tension or delight in victory

"Getting to Know Me"

John, a retired cardiologist, consulted me several years after the death of his wife, Alice. He had nursed Alice through four years of terminal illness. John had always been devoted to her and their children although he was too busy to spend much time with them.

After the children were born, he and his wife had never been able to recapture the romance of their courtship. She was more interested in the house and children than in John and his work. John and Alice never became close friends but they treated each other respectfully and never argued in front of the children. Alice had discreetly avoided any confrontations with him about his intermittent affairs, although he knew she was aware of them.

The women John had affairs with were young, attractive and could make intelligent conversation. It was flattering to win their affection and was an exciting diversion from the stress of work and mundane family problems. He did care for each of these women, but John said there was never any question that he loved his wife, never would have left her for any of them and believed she understood that commitment.

John was an intelligent and logical man, proud of his practical, no-nonsense approach to life. Even in retirement, his conscientious pragmatism was paying off handsomely in his management of investments. But lately he had become less and less interested in his business affairs or any other aspect of his life.

John's internist told him he was in good physical health at his age, but recommended that John talk to someone about his depression. A couple of John's friends suggested he let an expert help him out of the doldrums. John had been reluctant to seek counsel from anyone, let alone a psychiatrist. John called me when he caught himself ruminating about death. He realized he no longer cared whether a car hit him while he was jogging, as long as he died instantly and painlessly.

Indifference to his own death surprised and appalled John. He had always fought to preserve the lives of his patients and boldly taken on challenges in his own life. Yet, despite his many creative and interesting projects, he had become dissatisfied with life. For the first time, he couldn't get control of his feelings.

I suspected John was terribly lonely but unable to label the feeling. Searching for evidence, I asked him about his personal life. John told me about Susan, a woman he cared about and respected. John and Susan had dated exclusively for more than a year. She had been his first serious involvement after his wife's death. Their relationship had ended three months before I first saw John.

John said Susan had "dumped" him because of his lack of openness, his need to control her and his attempts to buy her affection with gifts. He admitted he had ignored Susan's repeated warnings that the gifts and expensive evenings dining out, although exciting at first, had begun to make her uncomfortable. John thought Susan was just being polite when she said that these lavish things were unnecessary. After all, John's competence and success were what he felt he had to offer, and he wanted to share them with someone he loved.

But Susan was a widow with modest tastes, accustomed to an unpretentious style of living. She would have preferred to spend a peaceful, relaxed time by themselves getting to know each other better. John had never spent much time getting to know people beyond what was necessary to impress them—he knew his wife just well enough for her to marry him, his patients just enough for them to let him treat them, business associates just enough to convince them to make deals, other women just enough to have affairs with them. John had difficulty understanding what people were saying when feelings were involved.

John gave me a rational analysis of his mental state: "You see, I feel like I've done it all and had it all. I've been successful in two careers and am wealthy far beyond my needs. I had a long and happy marriage. I have three decent and loving children, even if they are somewhat more dependent and less ambitious than I'd like. Maybe if I weren't around to take care of them, they'd be better off. I've traveled all over the world—to China and Africa this past year with Susan. I can't think of anything I haven't done that I'd like to try."

Throughout his narration, John showed no emotion—no regret at the break-up with Susan and no grief about his wife's death. When I commented on the absence of any obvious feelings about these painful events, John admitted that losing Susan had hurt him, but that his wife had been so ill for so long that it was a relief when she died. Then he added ruefully, "You may think I'm an unfeeling person, but that isn't true. I care but I just don't show it. I have strong feelings at times. I mean, everyone complains about my temper."

John went on to say he still felt some lust at times, but increasingly sex had become merely a biological urge. Intercourse, he observed dryly, now provided him the kind of relief he felt with urination and defecation. It certainly wasn't worth living for.

I explored his feelings about his children and grandchildren. I spoke of the love I felt for my two-year-old goddaughter Sarah—the sweet smell of her skin and my delight in getting her to laugh by tossing her in the air and catching her.

John smiled kindly, but with a hint of tolerant condescension at my ingenuous self-disclosures. He explained that despite his intellectual appreciation of what I was saying, he could not remember ever feeling the kind of inner warmth I was describing, at least not with the intensity I apparently experienced.

We all come by who we are for good historical reasons. To John, love was a matter of protectiveness, loyalty and possession. In his extramarital affairs, romance and lust were additional features. But lacking a compassionate sense of his own tender feelings, he couldn't empathize with others. When people he loved were hurting, he felt it was his job to make everything better. He would never merely hold and console them. John had no experience with comforting bad feelings and therefore had no idea how helpful comforting could be. He cringed at the idea of crying in someone else's arms.

John said his parents were sophisticated people. His father was an attorney and his mother a physician who, despite her professional education, had been a timid and overprotective mother. Their home was an orderly place where no one showed strong feelings except for his father who would yell at his wife occasionally and his sons frequently. There was anger, but no loud laughter and few tears.

When John or his brother would complain about their

father's severe punishments for minor transgressions, their mother would ask them to try to understand that their father meant well and just wanted them to be the best they could be. "Besides," she would add, "you know how hard he works and how difficult it is to be an attorney." The implied message was: "You should keep your pain to yourselves because it upsets me terribly and your father has more important problems to deal with."

John recalled an episode which occurred just after his thirteenth birthday. The entire family went to the movies and John was given money to purchase everyone's tickets. He returned with all the tickets except his own. He explained proudly that he needed another 25 cents since he was no longer "twelve and under." When John refused to go back and lie about his age, his father became enraged. (George and the cherry tree be damned!) Humiliated and furious, John tried to run away, but his father ran after him, slapped him and told him to stop acting like a child.

John's feelings were frequently crushed, but he was an excellent student and learned from the lessons of his childhood. He was taught that his feelings and sense of right were unreliable, usually wrong and best ignored, impressing and pleasing others is what gets you ahead, winning is all that counts and success is the name of the game.

Now John sat across from me. Although physically healthy and successful, he felt lonely, empty and resigned to death. To John, it seemed far easier to die than to cry and be comforted. Like many American males, to John, strength and masculinity meant being in control and unemotional. John's uncomforted pain and loneliness, his unexpressed warmth and tenderness, were so toxic all bottled up inside him that his spirit was ready to give up.

Imagine the fulfillment and well-being John would have experienced had he been able to read his feelings and the feelings of others. What if he had been open about his loneliness and grief at his wife's death? What if he had been able to appreciate what Susan needed and was asking for instead of trying to impress and control her? What if he had learned from her to feel, interpret and share feelings?

If John were as adept at handling feelings as he was at interpreting electrocardiograms and analyzing the stock market, his material success wouldn't have felt so empty. Sex might have been a delicious celebration of love instead of an intermittent itch that needed scratching. He might have had intimacy and fulfillment and been eager for what the future had in store. (But would he have been less successful? Perhaps, but not necessarily. Being able to handle feelings isn't a formula for failure. And financial success isn't all it's cracked up to be.)

Escape Route
Exposing the Trap

A portrait of someone in *The "Feelings Are Foolish" Trap* is like a caricature of practical thinking. It represents the extreme rationalist position: "If there's a problem and it's possible to solve it, do. If not, there's no sense crying about it. Just forget it and move on." By subordinating feelings to rational thinking and by suppressing strong emotions, you never have to feel too bad.

People caught in this trap are pseudo-mature. They seem to have accepted as gospel the parental admonition to cut out silliness, laughter and tears, to stop the childishness, grow up and act adult. As a result they can relax and play only if they are intoxicated or sneaking their pleasures.

Traditionally, the Chinese haven't differentiated between heart and mind. But Western thinking has dichotomized the mind and subjugated emotions to reason, ignoring the role of emotions in mental processes (such as memory and creative thinking). Rationalists point to the success of science, technology and business to support their argument. Yet most major breakthroughs in science and technology have come from serendipitous discoveries and from irrational, intuitive hunches.[1]

Even in business, people have begun to recognize that reason alone cannot make money. Hence the flood of people-oriented approaches to management in recent years.

The purely objective-rationalist position is woefully inadequate for understanding human behavior and relationships. Because feelings do not follow the usual rules of logic, they can't be managed within a purely rational problem-solving approach. However, once you learn to decipher their code, your feelings begin to make sense. They become as understandable and manageable as most external phenomenon.

Uncontrolled feelings are disruptive and even destructive. But there are two kinds of control of feelings:

1) *The "Feelings Are Foolish" Trap* control in which strong feelings are considered messy and unnecessary:

> To get control of my life I must ignore my feelings and let reason guide every decision. If my emotions are interfering with logical thinking, I have to do something to get rid of them right away.

2) A healthier control, free of Mind Traps:

> I must listen to my feelings to understand their message and then guide my actions by taking that message into consideration. In order to feel right, I must learn to read my feelings as accurately as skilled pilots read their instruments.

The calm protection from self-doubt provided by *The "Feelings Are Foolish" Trap* is purchased at an exorbitant

[1]*Edison's discovery of the light bulb is a good example of the former; Einstein's relativity theory, of the latter.*

cost. You can't play and feel joy if you've learned to suppress strong feelings. And intimacy is impossible if you are unable to understand another person's thoughts and feelings.

Feelings can be considered the musical emanations of the human spirit. The tune is sometimes sad and mournful, sometimes harsh and dissonant, sometimes serene and peaceful, sometimes light and playful and sometimes carefree and elated. If you stifle feelings, you suffocate the spirit and never hear the music.

Reason without the counterbalance of emotion creates an inner void and an insatiable compensatory craving for material rewards like wealth, power and prestige, which ultimately turn out to be unfulfilling. If you need to rest, to play or to be hugged, an extra day of work (no matter how productive) won't take care of your need. Only after your spirit's requirements for nurturing and respect have been sufficiently satisfied can material rewards become a fulfilling bonus. (See Chapter 19, *The Great American Success Trap.*)

The "Feelings Are Foolish" Trap originates in childhood. To prevent it, adults need to pay greater attention to the comforting of children. Only if children are reassured that emotional hurt is an unavoidable part of life will they be able to learn healthy attitudes toward emotional discomfort. Parents' concern for feelings—their children's and their own—validates feelings as important messages worth understanding. And since feelings come from the core of a person, if you validate feelings, you validate the person.

Comforted and respected children become comforting and respectful adults. Because they can accept comforting for themselves, they don't have to assiduously avoid ever getting hurt and thus they can risk intimacy. They can use a balanced consideration of heart and mind to guide their lives.

Feeling bad and needing comforting are not signs of

defectiveness, weakness or foolishness. Nothing is more human than to be vulnerable, to feel hurt and to need comforting. And nothing is more mature than to accept responsibility for your spiritual well-being.

A New Direction

Readers who wish to rid themselves of this trap need to pay attention to their emotional pain and then learn to find and accept comforting for it. For guidance, see Chapter 6, *The "Bad Feelings Are Wrong" Trap: A New Direction,* pp. 68–69, and Part 4, *Handling Feelings.* For more on rest and play, see Chapter 24, *Well-Being: The Goal of Personal Change.*

PART 4

Handling Feelings

CHAPTER 8

Guidelines for Handling Feelings

Feelings are irrational, amorphous and confusing. They don't speak clearly. Feelings can affect how you act even when you aren't aware of them. How you handle your feelings largely determines the quality of your life.

Ways of Handling Feelings

There are three major ways to handle feelings:

1. You can deny, ignore and suppress them.

2. You can react unthinkingly to feelings—for example, by withdrawing when hurt or attacking when angry.

3. You can learn to monitor your feelings, compassionately examining them in order to understand what they reflect about the condition of your spirit. You can use this information to help make decisions.

Suppression, the first approach to feelings listed above, is a way to avoid experiencing feelings. People in *The "Feelings are Foolish" Trap* subdue their emotions in this way. They rely exclusively on intellect to run their lives and miss the vital contribution feelings can make. Denying feelings may buy protection from emotional pain, but the price is high. If you dull negative feelings you can't fully experience positive feelings like joy, tenderness and love. And even if you try to suppress strong feelings, they will affect your decisions in illogical destructive ways.

In the reflexive approach, feelings get expressed with little control or modification. This is the way a young child or lower animal acts. "Go with your feelings" was the short-sighted and dangerous advice offered by pop-psychologists during the 1960s and 70s. Were people to simply follow their feelings without discrimination, many would find themselves in jail for assault.

Only in the third approach, monitoring feelings, is intellect used to full advantage in the analysis and orchestration of feelings. Human consciousness makes it possible for us to treat feelings not only as experiences but also as important information we can use to make choices in day-to-day life.

Feelings: A Nonverbal Code

Feelings are nonverbal messages which you must learn to interpret. There are an infinite variety of feelings. Think of a person you see on a day-to-day basis who is important to you. Consider how many different moods and attitudes you can discern in that person merely by observing his or her facial expressions.

Though you may also be able to recognize numerous feelings within yourself, they are usually difficult to put into words and explain to others. Words fail us more in the description of feelings and bodily sensations than anywhere else. But becoming more precise about labeling and identifying feelings can help you enjoy a better life.

A wine connoisseur's skill at making subtle taste, color

and odor distinctions enables him to better appreciate wine drinking; a music aficionado's knowledge of the intricacies of a particular form of music heightens her experience of the music. In a similar way, increased awareness and sophistication about your feelings can enhance every aspect of your life. If you join intellect and emotions into a partnership, you can work towards intimacy and well-being.

Handling Feelings: Art, Not Science

Feelings are experiences. And experiences will *never* be measured objectively. No matter how proficient scientists may become at determining what's happening chemically in a person's brain while he or she is feeling a particular emotion, they will never know for certain what an emotion feels like when someone else is feeling it.[1]

Because feelings are subjective, they have been relegated to a subordinate role in our materially oriented culture. The human spirit suffers as a result of this neglect. Although we can't be clear in describing feelings and although feelings aren't objective or rational, they deserve our careful attention because how we feel has everything to do with the quality of our lives. Proficiency in understanding feelings is vital to making difficult decisions and achieving self-acceptance.

The spirit, the needy and sensitive child within you, cannot take care of itself. It is incapable of mature and rational

---

[1]*The world's leading behaviorist, B. F. Skinner, recently outlined a "science of feelings"* (Times Literary Supplement, May 8, 1987, p. 489). *By definition science relies on the objective. So a science of feelings is a contradiction in terms. We have as much need of a science of feelings as a science of music, painting or poetry. What we do need is to develop the art of handling feelings. This requires an experiential inquiry, not an objective, experimental one as Skinner is proposing. To better understand the meaning of various feelings, we must refine the words we use to label them. A more complete and precise language for feelings would improve our relationships with ourselves and each other.*

judgment. It cannot be relied upon to make decisions. Yet its needs, vulnerabilities and intuitions must be taken into consideration if you are to live well. And it is primarily through feelings that your spirit speaks to you. Most people have difficulty understanding themselves because they are uneducated and confused about the meaning of feelings. The next two chapters are devoted to looking at what particular feelings are saying to you about the condition of your spirit. They are intended only as a sampling of the possibilities for understanding feelings. Feelings are a great and poorly explored frontier. In a world only a button push away from nuclear holocaust, the future may depend on the successful exploration of this frontier.

Basic Principles in Handling Feelings

- Feelings contain important information, but they should not be trusted implicitly or blindly.

- Conversely, feelings are never ridiculous or wrong and thus should not be ignored.

- Feelings speak in a nonverbal code that requires deciphering to be understood.

It is useful to stand back from negative feelings. When you feel bad, a serious but common mistake is to ask, "What's wrong with me that I feel so bad?" Just as useless is the opposite question: "What's wrong with the other person who's making me feel bad?" It is more helpful to determine what your feelings are telling you and how you can modify your behavior to feel better.

Positive feelings should be handled differently. It's a mistake to question positive feelings while you have them. Good feelings, like the mouths of gift horses, are best left unexplored, and should simply be enjoyed. But once good feelings have run their course, it's worth reflecting on the conditions that made those good times possible.

The more you feel good, the more you will become addicted to feeling good and the more intolerant you will become about feeling bad once the unfamiliarity of feeling good begins to wear off. Eventually *The Familiarity Principle* (see Chapter 3) comes into play in a positive way. Bad feelings become signals for you to try to do something to feel better.

Pain, physical and emotional, is the most basic negative feeling, yet emotional pain often goes unrecognized, hidden behind nervousness, fear, anger, resentment, guilt, shame or jealousy.

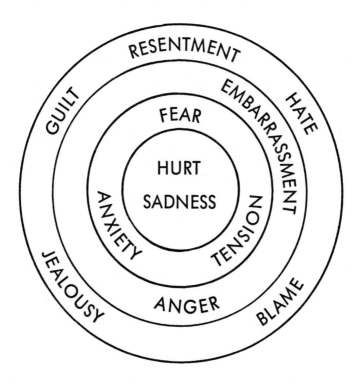

Handling Uncomfortable Feelings
Step-by-Step Guidelines

1. Regard your uncomfortable feelings as coded messages to be deciphered.

2. Stand back from yourself and consider each aspect of your current life: each important relationship, your work, your requirements for rest, recreation and growth.

3. As you consider each aspect of your life, identify the source of your uncomfortable feelings by noting which aspect of your life causes you the most discomfort. Find the fear and hurt behind more complicated feelings such as guilt, anger, resentment, embarrassment, jealousy or blame.

4. Try to feel compassion for yourself and your pain. Be understanding to the vulnerable and hurt child within you.

5. Do something to improve your situation. Experiment with ways of earning more self-respect and of getting the comforting you require from others. You may need to be held. Perhaps you need to be candid, fair but firm, with whomever you feel is treating you badly. If nothing else, at least write down how you feel and talk to someone who is likely to understand and care.

CHAPTER 9

Hurt, Sadness and Fear

Hurt

Recently, a client yelled at me. I had been talking on and on while she politely but impatiently waited to tell me something. Her anger made me feel bad for hours after the session even though the incident blew over immediately.

I recall many episodes from childhood when my mother would suddenly lash out at me during a discussion. Then she'd storm off, slam her door, fasten the lock and turn on opera music. (I hated listening to opera until I was thirty-five, when I finally was able to feel compassion for how hurt and angry I felt during these episodes.)

Hurt reverberates inside me for hours after being angrily criticized, especially if I am criticized by a woman I respect. That vulnerability will be a part of me for as long as I live, no matter what I do or how well I understand its source.

All the understanding in the world won't erase your vulnerability, but a different attitude can help you handle your pain. New atittudes towards your feelings can greatly improve your relationship with yourself. Hurt becomes much more bearable when you're on your own side.

I discovered it was helpful to do the following each time I felt uncomfortable: stand back from my pain, recognize my sensitivity, look at my childhood to identify the wounds that increased my vulnerability, have more compassion for my pain and try to do something constructive to make myself feel better. Pain is most burdensome when endured alone. Telling a few people about a painful incident often helps. Knowing that someone understands and cares can reduce the severity of any pain. (The field of psychotherapy and counseling wouldn't exist otherwise.)

You can't change your feelings by a mere act of will. All you can change are your attitudes towards your feelings. More compassionate attitudes towards unpleasant feelings can reduce their intensity.

The following attitude towards hurt can be helpful:

There's nothing wrong with feeling hurt. My emotional pain only reflects my sensitivity. Just because I'm vulnerable and easily hurt doesn't mean I'm weak. Weakness is not just *feeling* pain; weakness is *letting pain defeat me.*

The better I am at finding people to comfort me regularly, the more pain I can handle. Comforting makes me stronger. I need to find a way to reduce my pain as constructively as possible. If I'm willing to hang in and endure the painful situation long enough to learn from it, I'll be less likely to get hurt in the future.

The worst emotional pain I can experience is to feel worthless. When I doubted myself, the pain of worthlessness was a lurking threat. When I experienced even minor losses, rejections or failures—a store clerk or a waiter being nasty—my pain would be severe and my self-doubt would increase. If I experienced a serious loss, I would fall into despair and give up.

Now I have accepted my worth. Loss, rejection and failure still hurt me. But my pain is sadness about the loss, not despair because I feel defective, worthless and meaningless. Grief is, to a degree, consolable. Despair about being defective is not.

Sadness and Grief

Sadness is the pain of loss. Once you have an emotional investment in something, that thing becomes a part of your identity and the loss of it can cause an identity crisis. When you lose someone or something you feel strongly about, you lose a part of yourself and must go through the stages of loss: disbelief, anger, sadness and gradual detachment. Even the loss of a long term enemy can be disruptive.

There is nothing to be done for sadness other than to go through the normal, purging, healing waves of grief with as much compassion for yourself and comforting from others as you can arrange. Comforting and the passage of time can gradually heal wounds left by loss. But if grief is stifled and comforting avoided, wounds will fester.

Sadness is an absolutely necessary and healthy emotion. To have a healthy spirit you must be able to grieve and be comforted. People with self-doubt who have difficulty accepting comforting learn to avoid caring too much about anything. Their spirits wither in the icy grip of hurt and loneliness.

A healthy attitude towards grief might be phrased in the following way:

My heart is aching with sadness. I feel empty inside. But it makes sense that I should be in pain. I cared so deeply and have lost so much. During waves of grief, I need to get as much comforting from others as I can arrange. In between the waves, I can try to live my life as fully as possible.

Crying and comforting are good for me. I feel better when I am comforted while I cry.

I know with help and time I'll heal. The waves of grief eventually will become briefer and farther apart. I know my life will never be quite the same. But I have more to see and do, to learn and offer once my grief passes. For now, grieving and healing are about all I can manage.

Occasionally, a feeling of sadness can come over you without apparent cause. However, with effort, you can usually identify what precipitated the feeling. Simply talking about the sadness out loud with yourself or with someone else may often be enough to figure it out. Writing your reflections in a private journal can also help. Something will have triggered this feeling, something associated in your mind with a loss: a smell, a song, the weather, a scene from a movie. Once you recognize the source, you can usually do something to alleviate the feeling, like talking to a person who understands you.

Fear and Nervousness

Who hasn't experienced the fear of loss, rejection and failure? Most students become tense before tests in school and then have exam nightmares later in life. What salesperson hasn't felt nervous about making an unsolicited call? Who can stand up before an audience and feel no apprehension?

Fear and nervousness are always related to the threat of being hurt. Fear may be a realistic and appropriate response to something, or it may be an overreaction provoked by a situation which poses little real danger. If, when you stand back and consider your fear, it seems to be an overraction, you will usually discover that the current situation reminds you of something severely painful in your childhood.

A helpful attitude toward fear and nervousness is:

> I can't prevent myself from feeling afraid and nervous. What I can do is step back from my feelings and carefully examine each aspect of my life. When I hit upon what is bothering me most, my feelings will let me know what the threat is. Once I have identified the threat, I can decide what steps I can take to reduce my discomfort.

> If what I fear is the impending loss of someone I love (for example, because of illness), I need to explain the fear and sadness I'm feeling to people who care about me, including the person I'm afraid of losing.

A Note on Courage

Courage is not a feeling. Like beauty, courage is only in the eye of the beholder. Courage is the act of doing what one feels is right despite one's fears. The greater the fear, the greater the courage necessary to overcome it and do the right thing. Where there is no fear, there can be no courage.

Many heroes reveal in interviews how frightened they were at the time of their heroic acts—some explain that they were so desperate they felt they had no choice; others were so inspired by the actions of others that they just joined in and helped out without a second thought; still others admit that they did what they did before they even had a chance to think; and there are some whose brave actions were a result of righteous indignation and rage. But you'll never hear a hero boast of feeling a surge of courage.

I have seen many frightened people wait for courage to arrive while they waste precious time suffering pain and loss of self-respect. They await the abatement of their fear and the onset of courage—to confront their wife, husband or boss, to look for a job, to go back to school. They will wait forever. The *feeling* of courage will never come because it doesn't exist. You are only courageous when you do what you feel is right despite your fear. Everyone feels fear, so everyone can be courageous.

What can help you to act courageously? *Inspiration* by the actions of others in similar situations and *desperation* about your own situation can be tremendously helpful.[1]

An excellent way to get accustomed to being courageous is to place yourself in unfamiliar and frightening situations which require you to learn and grow—such as participating in Outward Bound or Toastmasters, or traveling alone through an unfamiliar area—despite your fears of failure.

When you try new things you may be frightened. But afterwards you will feel a surge of self-respect and you will have gained competence and confidence. You will also have taken a step towards self-acceptance and the elimination of self-doubt.

---

[1] *The use of a combination of personal desperation, support from others and inspiration has helped make Alcoholics Anonymous a success.*

CHAPTER 10

Anger, Resentment, Guilt and Embarrassment

Anger

A thirty-year-old woman in the midst of her second divorce is currently consulting me. She left her doting first husband because he bored her. "There was no chemistry," she said. "He was devoted to me, but I had no romantic feelings for him. It became too uncomfortable to stay with him."

She left her second husband because he abused her. She now lives with her two-year-old daughter and their housekeeper. Although her second husband has very limited visitation privileges, she is obsessed by what she sees as his attempts to control her and poison the mind of their daughter.

I told her that divorced parents' efforts to denigrate their ex-spouses in hopes of winning their children's loyalty usually backfire. But my reassurances were useless.

This woman's self-doubt is extremely powerful. Unconsciously she feels undeserving and is therefore terrified of losing her daughter's love. Over-possessiveness towards her daughter and fury at her estranged husband distract her from her self-doubt and fears. Instead of treating her insecurity with compassion and acting in a way more likely to earn self-respect, she resorts to anger at herself "for being stupid enough to get involved with the guy in the first place!"

Anger can be an energizing force, useful in overcoming fear and earning self-respect. But anger can also be an addictive drug used to hide from self-doubt, a distracting stimulant to numb pain and to avoid doing what would be necessary to take care of the vulnerable and needy child inside.

Recognize that anger is always a reaction to hurt and fear. When you feel angry, look for the hurt and fear behind the anger. Who or what is the source of your anger, hurt and fear? How can you confront the situation in a constructive way that will increase your self-respect and relieve your discomfort?

The following attitude toward anger may be helpful:

I'm no longer willing to follow the habitual path of least resistance and smallest risk, blaming others or myself and getting depressed without doing anything to relieve my pain and improve my situation. It's almost always better to arrange for understanding and comforting of my fear and hurt than to simply vent my anger.

Sometimes my anger may be caused by frustration because I'm thwarted from getting what I want or because I'm being discriminated against. Sometimes it makes sense to feel upset. If I know why I'm upset I can do something constructive to try to remedy the situation—respectfully but firmly confront someone who's actions are painful to me, commit myself to taking care of some need I'm feeling, join an organization or demonstration, write a letter or donate money to a cause devoted to righting an injustice.

The difference between experience of a feeling and expression of it is crucial. The feeling of anger is a private message that requires examination and understanding instead of being thoughtlessly expressed. Sometimes expressing anger can be inappropriate or even extremely dangerous. But occasionally showing anger can help get another person's attention. Anger can help you to act courageously. Anger can make it possible to do what in your heart you know is right despite the risks.

Resentment

People are *angry* when someone hurts them. They are *resentful* if they don't try to do something about it. Resentment is the result of having put up with hurt for too long. Resentment allows you to avoid standing up for yourself. Resenting and complaining go hand-in-hand—neither does any good. If you merely complain instead of taking action, you will be resentful.

People resent the bullies they're afraid to confront, not those they've had the courage to fight. Even if you lose the battle, facing the person you're resenting will rid you of your resentment and increase your self-respect. A loss of self-respect always underlies resentment. You stop resenting when you start acting bravely on behalf of your inner child.

If you feel resentful, try the following attitude:

My resentment comes from putting up with unfairness, disrespect and lack of consideration for my feelings; from my willingness to "suffer the slings and arrows of outrageous fortune."

If I feel resentful, I have to admit to myself that I have

avoided taking any action to rectify what is hurting me. I've been afraid of the responsibility and what might happen if I were to attack the problem. It's been easier to grumble than to act.

I recognize that resentment poisons my spirit. I have to risk whatever is necessary to defend my spirit and improve my self-respect by confronting my boss, my wife, my husband, my parents, the government or whoever has hurt me.

Stale Resentment:

If I resent someone for what they did in the past, then I need to get it out of my system somehow. I should tell the person directly, not that he was wrong, but *how I feel* about what he did. It's not a matter of right or wrong. I just need to try to have my feelings recognized, understood and cared about.

If the person you resent is no longer around or has changed too much for you to tell them now, then it's worth at least writing to yourself what you feel or talking to someone about what you wish you'd said at the time. It's hard to fully appreciate your feelings unless you express them in a concrete way.

Guilt [1]

Despite chronic guilt, George, a retired school teacher in his late fifties, had been unable to give his mother the time

[1] *Guilt and embarrassment are the opposite of self-respect. They reflect the spirit's discomfort with one's own thoughts, feelings and especially actions. Guilt is the anger at oneself and the fear of punishment one feels one deserves for one's wrong actions. Embarrassment is the desire to hide from others because of fear of being teased, criticized and socially ostracized for not being up to some standard. Thus a mother may feel guilty about yelling at her daughter, but is ashamed of not having prepared a report by the promised deadline.*

and caring she was pleading for in her irritating and indirect way.

George was also resentful of her past treatment of him and showed it in his behavior towards her. His mother had never been warm and comforting to him in his youth. She hadn't given him the approval and support he felt he had earned. Yet now, far too late as far as he was concerned, she told him and anyone else who would listen how much she adored him. Now that she was treating him better, George felt guilty about not doing the same for her.

George realized he could not allow his spirit to writhe in guilt and resentment. He could sense how his attitude towards his mother was poisoning his spirit. Fortunately he was learning to have compassion for himself, for what he had felt as a child and what he felt now.

George decided to offer his mother the kind of compassion and caring he wished she had provided him. He was able to offer love because he found a reason to be loving to her without hypocrisy. He began to be loving to her not out of a sense of obligation and not because he felt she had earned it, but because he realized that being loving to her would be a gift to himself as much as to her. His loving care finally released his spirit from its incessant, aching guilt.

Try the following way of managing guilt:

Guilt, like resentment, is a signal that I need to do something for my spiritual well-being. If I allow guilt to continue and don't take action to get rid of it, the guilt will become toxic and begin to destroy me. Prolonged guilt helps no one. It only gets in the way of compassionate healing actions.

Guilt protects me from having to live my life the best I can. As long as I feel guilty I can keep doing what I'm doing. But in the process of protecting me from making new mistakes, guilt prevents me from having new experiences and learning from them.

Guilt is often presumptuous. If I indulge in prolonged guilt I am implying I should be able to prevent all mistakes and bad things from happening.

Making amends or beginning to behave in ways I admire would be far better than wasting my time and further poisoning my spirit with self-criticism and guilt.

If I'm not willing to change, I must accept my guilt as the internal price I have to pay to keep doing what I feel guilty about. My guilt is an excellent sign. It should reassure me that I am a fundamentally good person and can't do what I know is wrong without feeling bad about it.

If my guilt is about something I'm doing now, I can get rid of it as soon as I'm ready to change. If I'm guilty about what is done and irreversible, I must search my heart to see what I can do to make amends and regain self-respect. I may never be able to erase the pain I feel for what I've done, but at least I can be proud of how I'm living *now*. To recognize I'm only human doesn't excuse my actions, but it should help me be compassionate to those—including myself— who are trying their best.

Self-doubt complicates guilt. If you doubt yourself, guilt will fit your negative sense of yourself: "I'm deficient in some way, so it makes sense that I do bad things. I should feel guilty and bad." Self-doubt and guilt flourish in each other's company. If you're worried you may be flawed, you'll believe you deserve to feel guilty. If you accept yourself, then guilt becomes a message to change something in your life.

Programmed Guilt

Rapid changes in cultural values may catch you in situations which seems acceptable given the current cultural climate, and yet may still *feel* wrong to you. If you feel guilty because you've been brought up to believe something is wrong, you'll end up feeling bad no matter what you decide to do.

For example, millions of single men and women in recent years, especially those middle-aged or older, have had to reexamine their feelings about cohabiting without marriage. Although society increasingly condones cohabitation and these people can think of many rational reasons to try it, they may still feel guilty about it. They may feel damned if they do decide to move in with someone, but feel lonely and disappointed if they don't. Feelings don't change merely because you want them to or because they are no longer consistent with the way you think.

Some people raised with strong prohibitions against homosexuality find themselves primarily attracted to people of their own sex. They often feel tortured by the incongruity between what they feel and what they have been brought up to believe. There are no simple and painless solutions for their dilemma. The price is severe either way.

You may find the following attitude helpful in trying to sort out programmed guilt:

Sometimes I feel guilty about things I do or am considering doing even though I don't honestly think that doing them would be wrong. I feel guilty because of the values I was taught in childhood. There's nothing I can do about this guilt except stand back from myself and have compassion for my discomfort.

I need to recognize how difficult it is to free myself of childhood brainwashing. I have to remind myself that I can't directly change my feelings. *I can only change my attitudes and actions despite how I feel.* I can use my intellect to understand the message of my feelings. Then I must decide whether I will yield to programmed guilt or whether I will do what I feel is right and find a way to deal with the guilt.

Inappropriate Guilt

Like the word "love," the word "guilt" covers a wide variety of feelings. You may say you feel guilty. But if you carefully examine your feelings, you might discover you're being unfair to yourself. You may have done nothing wrong and the feeling could be more positive.

For example, I was driving down the highway with my wife when she commented that a particular stretch of road always stirred up her guilt about a horrible earache our daughter suffered almost two decades ago. On that night we had searched for an hour before we were able to find a 24-hour convenience store to buy some medicine. I remembered the incident but couldn't understand why my wife felt guilty. I asked her what we had done wrong. On reflection she realized she couldn't think of anything more we could have done to help. She just recalled how terrible she felt being unable to relieve our daughter's pain. My wife misidentified her feelings as guilt instead of loving concern.

People often use the word "guilt" too glibly and misunderstand themselves as a result. Negative feelings especially need to be closely examined and carefully labeled. They are not always what they seem.

Embarrassment

A physician consulted me about his procrastination in his work. I began by exploring his feelings about his current job. His career had been going well. He worked as a full-time researcher at the university and was regularly promoted. His research was well-funded and he had earned some prestige in his field. Yet his enthusiasm had waned. He was procrastinating more and more and felt as if he were just going through the motions.

I asked him whether he thought he was wasting his time and energy on his current projects. He seemed taken aback, but then looked relieved and agreed that I might be right. Apparently his work had not been giving him any real satisfaction for quite some time. But he had not taken a step back from himself to see whether he felt proud of his efforts. He wasn't challenging himself and thus felt no self-respect. No wonder he had no sense of well-being. Once he began to sort out his feelings, he was ashamed of himself. His embarrassment helped him redirect his efforts to more challenging and meaningful teaching and research.

The next time you feel ashamed, ask yourself if you're ashamed about your efforts or the results of your efforts. Are you ashamed of *how* you have gone about doing something or *what* you have done?

Then consider adopting the following attitude:

> If I'm ashamed of my efforts, then my embarrassment is a valuable message. It means I have to try harder. But if I've done my best and still fallen short of my expectations, then it's time either to revise those expectations or find out a better way to do what I'm trying to do. Perhaps my expectations are unfair. Maybe I want results as a way of impressing myself and others in order to get rid of self-doubt. But excellent results will never be enough to earn self-acceptance. All I can do is to try my best. I can be in control of my efforts but not results and not others' reactions to my efforts.

Even worse than embarrassment about results is

embarrassment about things over which I have no control—like my physical attributes or my family's background. I need to have compassion for myself when I feel embarrassed about things I can do nothing about. Instead of being preoccupied with my weaknesses, I must begin to concentrate on my strengths and on making the most of the rest of my life. (See *The Prove Your Worth Traps,* Part 8.)

PART 5

The Fear of
Change Traps

CHAPTER 11

The "Biased Against Myself" Traps

"O wad some Power the giftie gie us
To see oursels as ithers see us!"

Robert Burns

Compare and Despair Trap:

"When I compare myself with others I usually come out the loser. They're as good as they seem; I'm as bad as I feel."

"I find it hard to believe you don't know
The beauty you are
But if you don't
Let me be your eyes
. . . I'll be your mirror
Reflect what you are
In case you don't know."

Lou Reed

The "You Flatter Me" Trap:

"Thanks for the compliment, but I'm afraid you're mistaken. You don't know me the way I do."

Commonly Associated Features

People in *The "Biased Against Myself" Traps* might have some of the following characteristics:

- fear of not being good enough

- anxiety when things are going well

- tendency to idealize and idolize others

- tendency to be a workaholic and overachiever but unable to enjoy success

- tendency to procrastinate and underachieve

- reluctance to expose true feelings

- inability to accept comforting except when in extreme pain

- pessimistic and cynical outlook on life

- tendency towards self-blame

The Grass is Always Greener . . .

Lawrence is a world class physicist and a professor. He has made millions in private industry. He has traveled around the world as a consultant and speaker. Lawrence's wife, Janice, is a respected physician in the field of neonatal pediatrics and also happens to be beautiful.

I admit Lawrence and Janice are not an average couple, more like soap opera characters than real people. But extreme examples can be useful to illustrate a point—in this case that people with self-doubt, even those most blessed by nature and circumstance, often reinforce their negative self-concept by ruthlessly comparing themselves to others and deftly side-stepping compliments.

Lawrence would only stop working when he fell asleep from exhaustion. And he never stopped worrying. He worried whether he was doing the right thing, whether other people were critical of him, whether some day he might lose all he had made, and whether he would eventually be exposed as just a medicore overachiever. He envied his colleagues' apparent confidence. They always seemed on top of their work. They satisfied their commitments and met their deadlines.

But despite his admiration for the people he thought were better than he was, Lawrence didn't try to emulate them. Instead he used them as weapons against himself. By focusing on their strengths, he could highlight his own defects and confirm that he was lacking something.

Many people admired Lawrence and told him so—how creative and enterprising he is, how much enthusiasm and energy he has. But these honest observations made him uncomfortable. He felt he had just been lucky. Despite his accomplishments, money and other people's respect, Lawrence felt inferior and unhappy.

Vivian is another example of someone who compares and despairs. When I met her she was thirty-eight and beautiful, a study in elegance. My secretary, Jan, once commented that Vivian seemed to have stepped right out of the pages of *Vogue.* I always felt vaguely uncomfortable around her, as if I should go home, shower and change into something more stylish before returning to her presence.

Not that Vivian was critical of me or anyone else. In fact, she couldn't have been more polite, gracious and anxious to please. What unnerved me was her perpetual poised and posing manner, as if she were constantly getting ready to have her picture taken.

Vivian's second husband was extremely wealthy, a naturalized citizen rumored to be involved in international weapons trade. Vivian saw it as her responsibility and public role to lighten the shadow cast by her husband's odious reputation. She filled her days doing charity work in the community and her evenings entertaining the socially prominent.

Vivian was a superb chef and hostess. Invitations to her dinner parties were cherished, not only for the social notoriety they guaranteed but also for the gustatory delights they provided. She was a conservator of a disappearing art form: exquisite continental dining in the home.

Reputed to have everything one could ask for, Vivian nonetheless saw herself as a well-disguised impostor. She felt that her family background was embarrassingly middle-class. She saw her education and fund of knowledge as woefully inadequate—just enough to make polite, superficial conversation. Despite regular visits to famed health spas, plastic surgery and the guidance of her private conditioning coach, Vivian was painfully aware of her losing battle with age. She resented younger women with tighter, more voluptuous bodies. And she knew her marriage was a pathetic facade. She had never loved her husband and despised the way he made and multiplied his fortune.

Vivian recognized that many other women envied her. Her preoccupation was to create the image of perfection which provoked their jealousy. Yet she pined for the wholesome, simple life she imagined other women had—a down-to-earth husband with an honest job and solid values, someone who enjoyed spending time with his wife and children.

Rejoicing in one's blessing is incompatible with *The Compare and Despair* and *The "You Flatter Me" Traps.* Despite Lawrence's and Vivian's wealth and their confident public demeanor, the void of self-doubt negated any possibility of real joy and satisfaction. Vivian and Lawrence are unusual examples. But how many of us are free of this self-defeating tendency to measure ourselves unfairly against others? How many of us can believe and rejoice in the compliments we receive?

Escape Route
Exposing the Trap

The Compare and Despair Trap and *The "You Flatter Me" Trap* are a self-defeating waste of time and energy. These *Biased Against Myself Traps* are prominent members of the Mind Traps which reaffirm one's self-doubting identity.

The Compare and Despair Trap acts in concert with *The Self-Doubt Trap* and *The "Bad Feelings Are Wrong" Trap* to deliver a knockout blow to one's sense of worth: "I feel bad, so I must be bad. Other people seem better than me. This assures me that I am who I've always believed I am— someone who is somehow deficient."

The Compare and Despair Trap is a key part of a toxic belief system in which life is seen as a competition to prove one's worth by demonstrating one is better, or at least not worse, than others. It could be argued that America's economy is fueled by this competitive "top-dog" attitude based on insecurity about ourselves: What is everyone wearing these days? What's the latest in stereos, careers and diets? Who's ahead—us or the Russians?

The Compare and Despair Trap reflects our culture's obsession with the external and material and its devaluation of the internal and spiritual. The error results from confusion between packaging and content, objective appearances and subjective *experiences* and other people's public demeanor with one's own private feelings and beliefs. Except for intimate friends (and perhaps hairdressers and therapists), no one has accurate information about what another person thinks and feels.

Born and bred in a materialistic atmosphere, it's easy to be deceived into believing you have to be rich and famous to enjoy a fulfilling life. You may forget that these are contrived games and rewards. If society's ideals accurately reflected the priorities of the human spirit, then most people, especially the so-called winners at these artificial games, would have less painful and more gratifying lives.

Need we look further than the apparently glamorous and fortunate public lives of the rich and famous belied by the scandalous and tragic revelations about their private sufferings? Many people are so dismayed by the suicide of attractive, talented wealthy people that they refuse to believe it. It is too threatening for many people to accept that the pot of gold at the end of the rainbow—success—frequently turns out to be a toilet. Successful people who come to a bitter end provide some self-doubting people with a reason to rejoice: "What a relief! Some of those people who look so much better than me are even worse off than I am."

Comparisons with others divert you from the search for self-respect. This search requires you to do what feels right and try for your personal best, instead of worrying about what others are doing.

The mission to stay ahead or at least keep up with everyone else ultimately fails. Self-doubt has such a powerful distorting effect that even if you become extremely successful, self-doubt will prevail. You'll just keep searching until you discover someone who makes you look inferior by comparison. You can always find people who seem better off in some important way. And you're always more likely to pay attention to those people who excel in those very attributes which you sense you lack most and therefore admire most. (Gifted people are more likely to receive compliments and adulation than others. Yet many gifted people suffer more from *The Compare and Despair Trap* and *The "You Flatter Me" Trap* than those who are less talented.)

Lawrence, the physicist described at the beginning of the

chapter, didn't feel worthy of being called a "multi-millionare," although he was one several times over. "I don't feel *that* rich," he said. "It's the people with more than twenty million who really impress me."

Dismissing other people's compliments of you is as destructive as comparing and despairing. Refusing to accept others' appreciation of you insults them as well as yourself. Your disagreement with their praise says they are wrong about what they think and feel. By rejecting their complimentary observations, you keep them at a distance. Your refusal to give up your bias against yourself keeps you lonely, self-centered and stuck in self-doubt. Compliments, after all, are not easy to come by. Why not appreciate them?

The Compare and Despair Trap and *The "You Flatter Me" Trap* support the foremost principle of human behavior, *The Familiarity Principle:* People cannot tolerate being treated in unfamiliar ways for long, even if these new ways seem logically preferable. People in *The Compare and Despair Trap* select people with whom they can adversely compare themselves in order to reinforce their negative identities. People in *The "You Flatter Me" Trap* refuse to consider the possibility that the compliments they receive may paint a more accurate picture than their own familiar sense of themselves.

But endless efforts to confirm self-doubt are only half the story. If ycu employ traps that confirm or reinforce self-doubt like *The Compare and Despair Trap* and *The "You Flatter Me" Trap,* you must compensate by continually searching for reassurance that although you're not that great, you're not all that bad either. On the one hand you don't want to lose your familiar identity, but on the other hand you don't want to feel defective.

When you have a toothache you keep touching the tooth partly in the hope that it has recovered and partly to reaffirm that it hasn't. In the same way, you keep trying to look good but always notice people who look better than you to confirm your negative sense of yourself. You discount compliments because you think you've fooled people by trying so hard to look good. Yet if you see someone who looks good, you criticize yourself for being inferior.

Modest refusal of compliments is so socially acceptable that people who are uncomfortable with compliments need only learn to *appear* appreciative, as if they have been given an undeserved and far too generous gift. Other people's positive observtions about you are important information worth your careful consideration. *The Biased Against Myself Traps* make it impossible for you to appreciate these invaluable insights about yourself. Ruminating about your inferiority lets you avoid the positive but frightening identity crisis *necessary* for constructive change. The enemies of self-respect, growth and well-being are fear, self-doubt and your familiar identity.

A New Direction

Try adopting a healthier attitude:

Maybe I've grown up believing there's something wrong with me and I feel like a hypocrite when I act any other way.

Maybe I've been given special gifts in certain areas. Maybe I'm a good person with a great deal to offer despite my weaknesses and faults. Maybe I've been afraid to accept my gifts because they feel like too much responsibility. If I accepted my strengths and talents then I would have to decide how to make the most of them.

Life is an opportunity to discover what I have to offer the world and what the world has to offer me. The chance of a lifetime is to discover and refine my true self. I need to do my best with what I was given and not bemoan what I lack. If I'm alert to opportunities and fortunate, my efforts can produce fulfilling results and rewards. At the very least my enthusiastic efforts will guarantee me self-respect.

When people compliment me, I must find the courage to consider the possibility that they're right about me, no matter how awkward and uncomfortable their admiration makes me feel. They don't suffer from my biases and misunderstandings about myself. So perhaps they can see some truths about me better than I because I've been too close to my discomfort to see myself clearly.

I know it's impossible to avoid comparisons entirely. Besides, there are advantages to looking at others. Everyone has something to teach me. I can use the good things about people I admire to inspire me. I can use their negative qualities to dissuade me.

Even some competitiveness can be helpful. Competing with my own past performances and the performance of others in similar situations can bring out the best in me, as long as I don't *have* to win in order to feel good about myself. Why not learn from others who are better than me at something instead of merely comparing myself unfavorably? I can't be the best or even good at everything, but I can use *my* talents well.

Why not trust the opinions of those who admire and love me? Why not *do* my best instead of having to *be* the best and refusing to believe anything but the worst.

Every time you catch yourself comparing yourself unfavorably with someone else, shift your thinking immediately and concentrate on finding something you can do that very day to make you proud of yourself.

When people pay you compliments, write down what they said as soon as possible. Then honestly consider the possibility that their opinions are accurate. You might benefit from keeping a file of compliments you've received to review when you're feeling down.

These changes will be difficult and awkward at first, but you can't get rid of negative attitudes about yourself without trying some positive ways of thinking and acting.

CHAPTER 12

The "People Don't Change" Traps

> "A wise man changes his mind, a fool never will."
>
> Spanish Proverb

The "I Can't Change" Trap:

"I am who I've always believed I am and there's no use trying to be different."

> "We are not the same persons this year as last; nor are those we love. It is a happy chance if we, changing, continue to love a changed person."
>
> W. Somerset Maugham

The "You'll Never Change" Trap:

"I know you're trying to change, but I'm afraid to be hopeful. You seem so awkward and phony when you try to be different. Sooner or later you'll go back to the way you were.

> "Blessed is he who expects nothing, for he shall never be disappointed."
>
> Alexander Pope

The "Seen One, Seen 'Em All" Trap:

"My experience proves that all men and women are alike. I know they'll disappoint me in the long run. There's no sense getting too close."

Commonly Associated Features

People with *The "People Don't Change" Traps* may have some of the following characteristics:

- easily upset by criticism
- reluctance to take on new responsibilities or try new things
- difficulty accepting comfort except when in extreme pain
- tendency to be opinionated and defensive
- need to be in control and right, or at least not wrong
- pessimistic and cynical outlook on life
- critical and blaming of themselves or others
- addictions to harmful people, substances or habits

Playing House

Doris consulted me because she was fed up with her husband's temper. She had heard that I was assertive and not easily intimidated. Doris said her husband had previously manipulated several therapists. This time she wanted someone her husband couldn't bully.

I've put up with Arthur's temper and abuse for too long and I'm not going to take it any more. [Doris sounded like the Peter Finch character in *Network.*] Either he begins to treat me properly, or I'm going to leave him. He says I'm just a hysterical female who keeps asking to be yelled at and insulted. When he's really mad he grabs me and shakes me.

For years he had convinced me that I was wrong. Finally I can see that he's the one with the problem. Just ask the people at his office. He's as bad with them as he is me. He's like a little kid. If he doesn't get his way he goes berserk. His mother tells me he's always been like that, just like his father.

In his first session with me, Arthur assured me he didn't need to ask what Doris had said. He said he had listened to her litany of complaints countless times.

Sure I lose my temper. You try living with constant complaining for twenty years and not get angry once in a while. But don't you believe the physical abuse crap. I've never struck her, though *she's* hit *me* before.

Look, I supervise a lot of people, many of them prima donnas. There's a lot of pressure in my work and Doris's nagging doesn't help. All I really want is a little understanding and support in my own home. You're not the first shrink we've seen, you know. Whenever we begin to make some progress she quits. I hope this time it'll be different but, quite honestly, I doubt it.

Over a period of a few months and about a dozen sessions, Doris and Arthur made some progress. Doris grudgingly admitted that Arthur had learned to control his temper. "But," she hastened to add, "it's obvious how hard he has to work at it. It's not like him to control himself. It seems so forced and artificial. I keep waiting for him to snap—or at least crack a tooth biting the bullet. He's hurt me too much for me to ever really trust him."

Arthur took a similar stance: "I grant you Doris has been off my back recently, but we're more like polite roommates than husband and wife. We're certainly no closer to being lovers. I think I'd get a warmer response if I were to try holding hands with a cop."

Arthur and Doris were afraid to let down their guard and be loving. Neither was willing to risk the rejection they believed would be forthcoming. Neither Arthur's nor Doris's parents had respectful and caring relationships. Arthur and Doris had never felt tenderness from each other. They were both lonely and starving for loving support, but couldn't accept comforting and had little experience offering it to anyone other than their children.

I wasn't able to help them find the compassion and courage necessary to risk intimacy with one another. Arthur's prediction about quitting therapy turned out to be accurate for both of them. Unfortunately, they terminated their consultations abruptly and well short of offering each other tenderness and understanding.

Doris had been attracted to Arthur because he was assertive and self-sufficient. He had been interested in her but was neither self-revealing nor physically demonstrative. He was someone she could try to win over, just as she had always tried to win love from her caring but emotionally reserved father.

Arthur, in turn, had selected Doris because she was smart, opinionated, critical and attractive—a woman who would look to him to fulfill herself and second-guess him at every opportunity. She had characteristics that evoked how he had felt as a child around his doting mother and critical father.

If Doris and Arthur were to provide each other the

respect, understanding and support they had always craved, they would have to risk suffering rejection and hurt. And if by some miracle one of them were to actually change permanently for the better, then the other would have to change also. They would be forced to become people they had never been, married to the kind of person they had never experienced. Few couples are open enough or desperate enough to enter willingly into that frightening void.

Too many marriages are like Arthur and Doris's, an unconscious collusion between two insecure people to perpetuate their childhood experience. By choosing someone who treats them in ways that feel familiar, they aggravate their emotional wounds and remain stuck in self-doubt. Mutual conformity to *The Familiarity Principle* helps couples avoid frightening and awkward changes. Unfortunately, few couples are willing to provide the warmth and understanding each partner needs to keep learning and growing. Fear and self-doubt can produce severe obstinacy.

Escape Route
Exposing the Trap

Change is impossible without deliberate and stilted efforts at first. Awkwardness in the process of changing is unavoidable. Acting differently in order to change and grow is not an attempt to deceive anyone. It is an attempt to transcend your lifelong identity.

Acting in new ways which you believe would increase your self-respect *will* feel artificial. Your familiar self resists change. The combination of awkward discomfort and increased self-respect is evidence you are making a courageous and determined effort to face the identity crisis required for significant change.

The "People Don't Change" Traps are cowardly capitulations to the status quo. These Mind Traps perpetuate the past and deny the possibilities within a person. Because people feel uncomfortable acting and being treated in unfamiliar ways, they tend to have fixed beliefs about themselves and to categorize one another according to past experiences. ("I'm lazy" or "You'll never understand me.") Labeling encourages the behavior they expect. Pigeonholing and denying the possibility of change allows them to pursue the habitual and lonely path of least resistance, a low-risk but dissatisfying life strategy that may feel safe but inhibits growth, excitement and intimacy. (See Part 6, *The Fear of Failure and Responsibility Traps.*)

Self-change is difficult. *But anyone can change. No one is inalterably destined to act in a certain way.* People are *not* "bad" or "just like so and so" unless we program them to be and unless they are unaware or refuse to believe that they have a choice. Most behavior is habitual and automatic but can become a matter of choice once you are aware of it and master the art of change. Anyone can change given enough understanding, time and effort.

In addition to unfamiliarity and fear, there is another powerful hindrance to change: the difficulty most people have believing they could ever really *think, feel,* and *act* like a different person than they are now.

A good example is Bob, who wasn't able to throw himself wholeheartedly into his father's business. He discovered he was afraid that if he became president of the company, he would use up the one dream he had nurtured his entire life. What would he live for then?

Bob lacked faith in his capacity to handle situations in whatever way would feel right to the person he would become at a later time. If you have enough practice treating yourself and others better, you begin to appreciate your spirit's ability to let you know what is right for you from moment-to-moment and you won't be afraid to be curious and experiment optimistically.

To change, you must be willing to try new attitudes and actions more likely to satisfy your needs and give you self-respect *despite your fears.* If you keep this up, you'll become someone who keeps growing, who is progressively more confident and more satisfied with life. Strange as it may seem, fear, awkwardness and self-respect are unavoidable along the path of self-change.

Discomfort isn't necessarily a bad thing. It's a message that needs to be heard and interpreted. Do you feel discomfort because you're acting in ways you feel are wrong, or because you're acting in new ways that are better but unfamiliar?

Couples can help or seriously interfere with each other's chances to grow. Change is often a painful, frightening process, especially when you aren't the person asking for the change. It's easy to get angry and blame your partner when you're uncomfortable, instead of asking for and offering comfort.

For example, I was upset when, after twenty years of marriage, my wife began traveling without me as part of her work. A great deal of forbearance on her part and my refusal to give in to my envy and resentment have enabled me to get to the source of my pain and find some solutions. By exploring my uncomfortable feelings, I eventually realized I had been assuming she and I would travel and discover different parts of the world together, as we always had. With her new job she would enjoy these experiences without me. That's a painful loss to me. Sharing the experience of traveling to new places has been one of the most satisfying aspects of our relationship.

Judy and I have worked out compromises and compensations for this significant change. For instance, she has learned to give me more warmth and appreciation in return for my support of her career. And as often as possible I go along as her assistant when she travels, a welcome relief from my usual position at center stage.

Discouraging your partner's efforts is a smokescreen for your own fear of changing. Since change is as inevitable in partnerships as in anything else, both partners must be willing to keep supporting each other's efforts or they will grow apart. If one partner changes, the other must also change or the relationship will disintegrate. People can either allow time and events to erode a relationship or they can take advantage of the discomfort each feels with the other's changes and use it as a challenge to discover and develop their own latent strengths.

A New Direction

For the basic attitude necessary to escape from this trap, see Chapter 4, *The Self-Doubt Trap: A New Direction,* pp. 47−48.

With a self-accepting attitude as a foundation, why not make life an exciting adventure of discovery guided by self-respect? Life without self-respect is empty. *Self-respect is the only thing in life entirely within your control.* It can be earned by trying to do what you feel in your heart is right.

The challenge is to suspend your worry that there may be something wrong with you and consider the possibility that there is nothing basically wrong and there never has been. Although it will be uncomfortable, you must find the courage to endure the identity crisis you must undergo if you really want to change. If you're uncomfortable the way you are, why not choose discomfort that at least offers the possibility of improving your sense of worth and self-respect?

If you want someone else to change, try adopting the following attitude about them:

The most effective means I have available is to change how I behave towards you. It's difficult to change my own attitude and behavior. But it's even more difficult for me to change yours.

If I could get you to change, your positive changes would mean I'd have to treat you differently and better anyway. So I'll take the initiative and treat you better right now. If I treat you with more respect, tenderness, consideration and encouragement, then it will be difficult for you to reject me as easily as you have.

Treating you with respect and compassion doesn't mean I have to tolerate abuse or hide my true feelings. I must treat you well and require you to treat me well.

And I must keep you current on exactly how I'm feeling about us. But I'll be careful how I say things. I just want you to understand how I think and feel, I don't want you to feel attacked and defensive.

I have to explain that I get hurt easily, especially by you, and I wouldn't be surprised if you're just as vulnerable to what I say and do. But just because we're easily hurt by each other doesn't mean either of us is intentionally *trying* to be hurtful. The great temptation when hurt and angry is to blame and retaliate. But blame and retaliation are destructive and block change. I'm interested in improving our relationship, not in winning or being right, ascribing blame or punishing you. (See Chapter 22, *The "I'm Right and You're Wrong" Trap,* and Chapter 14, *The Blame Trap.*)

We both experience the world in different ways. If we want more intimacy we need to educate each other about what we're thinking and feeling. I don't need you to agree with me as much as I need you to understand how I think and to care about how I feel, no matter how strange and unreasonable my thoughts and feelings seem to you. Imagine how close we'd feel if each of us became the world's expert on how the other thinks and feels?

Whatever I want from you is what I should offer you. Somehow I have to find the courage to overcome my fear of the pain I feel when you reject my loving gestures. Maybe if I explain how much your harshness hurts me, you might be willing to be gentle with me—especially if I commit myself to being just as careful with your feelings.

We must be lenient and forgiving of each other while we're trying to change. Neither one of us has had much experience with this new way of treating each other, so it's bound to feel awkward and frightening. We have to expect some backsliding and try not to pounce on mistakes and on retreats to familiar habits. As long as we see each other making honest efforts, no matter how awkward and unnatural, we need to be encouraging.

Fulfillment is a rare accomplishment in any endeavor. Fulfillment in relationships—intimacy—is especially difficult because it requires you to take responsibility for the demanding and sensitive child inside you, while also being responsive to the child inside the other person. It means negotiating for what you want, no matter how childish and unreasonable it seems, and offering the same in return. If you can accept the child within you and compassionately care for it, you'll have a more satisfying life.

Mind Traps block compassion because they're based on the assumption that one is flawed and undeserving. Only if Mind Traps are reduced does a nourishing partnership become possible. Only then can partners become friends who rejoice together in good times, provide comfort by sharing life's pain and support each other's efforts to grow. Admittedly, this ideal can be reached only intermittently even in the best of relationships. But intimacy every so often is infinitely better than none at all.

PART 6

The Fear of
Failure and
Responsibility
Traps

CHAPTER 13

The Fear of Failure and Success Traps

"He that lies upon the ground cannot fall."

Yiddish Proverb

The Fear of Failure Trap:

"If I tried, I'd probably fail. So why try? It's better to die a potential winner than a proven loser."

"We should not let our fears hold us back from pursuing our hopes."

John F. Kennedy

The Fear of Success Trap:

"Success builds expectations and makes disappointment worse when I fail. It's safer not to try too hard, get too good or have too much fun, love and success."

Fear of failure and success create a variety of excuses for not trying to do one's best.

"Live all you can; it's a mistake not to. It doesn't matter so much what you do in particular, so long as you have your life. If you haven't had that, what have you had?"

Henry James

"Where there is no hope there can be no endeavor."

Samuel Johnson

The "There's No Use Trying" Trap:

Stuck Without Choices: "I have to be where I am, with the person I'm with, doing what I'm doing—even though I don't really want to be."

Pessimism: "It's futile. No matter how well things are going, I know something will happen to ruin it. When something bad happens, it's evidence that things never work out in the long run. If something good happens, it just means I got lucky."

Cynicism: "Nothing I or anyone else does makes any real difference."

"It's Too Late": "What's the use of trying to change? I've already wasted too much time and I'd probably fail anyway. If I somehow were to become successful, I'd hate myself for not having started earlier."

Boredom: "Nothing interests me. I don't have anything valuable to offer the world and the world doesn't have anything to offer me."

Commonly Associated Features

People in the *Fear of Failure and Success Traps* may have the following characteristics:

- reluctance to commit themselves to anyone or anything
- tendency to procrastinate and have difficulty making decisions
- reluctance to take on new responsibilities or to try new things
- easily upset by criticism
- reluctance to expose true feelings
- anxiety when things are going well
- difficulty accepting honest praise
- tendency to be pessimistic, cynical, critical and blaming of themselves or others
- difficulty accepting comforting

Safe, But Sorry

Sy was an engineer whose job was going nowhere. He was forty and bored. He couldn't think of anything that would interest him.

Sy had been an ambitious dreamer in his college days. He had started off as an English major with aspirations of being a writer, but switched to engineering under pressure from his family to consider what they called a "practical profession." Since then he had bounced from job to job in product design. Although he would impress his superiors with flashes of creativity, he was unable to sustain his enthusiasm and follow through on any project.

From time to time Sy would enroll in a creative writing course. Invariably his teachers would encourage him to take his writing seriously since his worked displayed unusual talent. But Sy had the same difficulty committing himself to writing as he did to his engineering—he told me he had never finished any of the stories or scripts he started.

I tried confronting Sy: "You seem to work hard to make certain you remain mediocre at whatever you do. You manage to avoid failing, but you're careful not to excel either. You're the epitome of an 'A' potential, 'C' average underachiever."

Sy became irritated when I suggested that he held himself back by not trying his best. He asked me, "What makes you so certain I'm all that smart or capable? Most of the work I've been given could be accomplished by someone with a body temperature I.Q."

He could manage a deep commitment to only one thing: his low sense of worth. He couldn't accept that he was capable of high performance levels because they were inconsistent with his low self-concept. Sy admitted that he had never worked wholeheartedly all the way through a job. But he justified this by saying that he knew the finished product would be medicore. "My stuff is superficial. It has no real quality—all show, no substance. How can you keep up your enthusiasm when you can see better than anyone it's a bunch of crap?" I have never heard a more blatant example of someone projecting his identity onto his work.

Sy would try to impress people to compensate for his self-doubt but became uncomfortable when his achievements began to surpass his familiar self-doubting sense of himself. (See Chapter 3, *The Familiarity Principle.*) The he would relieve his identity crisis by unconsciously undermining his own efforts. Sy kept traveling this loop going nowhere and using his lack of progress to condemn himself.

Sy refused to consider the possibility that he was wrong about himself, that he might not be defective and might in fact be blessed. If he were to accept that there had never been anything wrong with him and appreciate that he had been given special talent, then he would have to take responsibility for using his talents well. If he wanted to accomplish a leap of faith in himself and his work, he would have to earn self-respect by experimenting whole-heartedly at something. He had never been willing to risk succeeding and raising people's expectations of him.

In a private session, Sy's wife described some of her frustrations with him. She hated his pessimistic and cynical attitude and his irritating habit of denigrating himself and anyone who complimented him. She told me: "If you're feeling low, he builds you up. If you're feeling good, he criticizes you. If you try to comfort him or give him an honest compliment, he makes you feel stupid. So I've given up being supportive when he's depressed."

Were we to accept Sy's negative premises about himself, we could appreciate how clever his cautious strategy was: If he tried enthusiastically and failed, then his worthlessness would be obvious. By not pushing himself too hard, he was able to avoid failure and still convince people he was pass-able. By maintaining mediocre efforts and results he had been able to conceal how flawed he feared he was. All his adult life, Sy had traveled this familiar mediocre turf, safe from success, failure, change and growth. If he played this cautious game well to the end, he could die with an unblemished reputation of having had great potential.

My urging him to stand back, be fair to himself and reevaluate the evidence of his life from a more compassionate perspective was simply too dangerous. Sy wouldn't risk opening old wounds.

In some ways, Sy was like Alex, the draftsman turned landscape architect who served as an example of *The "Bad Feelings Are Wrong" Trap* in Chapter Six. Both had severe self-doubt despite their talents. Both were afraid to commit themselves and try wholeheartedly. But Alex eventually was able to develop compassion for his emotional pain. He faced his fear of defectiveness and began to question it. He learned to accept his vulnerability and decided to go ahead and do the best he could, take pride in his efforts and accept the results, good or bad. Alex accomplished the leap of faith in his worth and is enthusiastic about himself, his family and his work.

Sy has been unable to do the same. He has no compassion for his own pain. To Sy, pain continues to be evidence of his defectiveness.

Alex is continually surprising himself by who he is becoming—he is surprised that he has intimacy in his marriage, that he has completed his education, that he is creative at what he does and that he has a delightful child of his own. Alex keeps growing by stepping off into the unknown, energized by his faith in himself and his curiosity about what he might become.

In contrast, Sy's life has no positive surprises. Sy consciously suspects what he has unconsciously been convinced of since childhood—that he is defective and incapable of accomplishing anything. Sy stays stuck in the past by continually recreating it. Everything he sees is distorted by self-doubt. Sy reaffirms his habitual view of himself by remaining stuck in Mind Traps.

Why was Alex able to find the courage to face his fear, pain and self-doubt while Sy still hasn't? I don't know. But the answer has wide implications for humanity. Anyone who can figure it out deserves a Nobel Prize.

Escape Route
Exposing the Traps

The Fear of Failure and Success Traps are ways people avoid the responsibility of discovering what they have to offer and of doing the best they can. If you have sufficient self-doubt, you won't take pride in your efforts, you'll interpret a failure as evidence of your defectiveness and you'll view every setback as a failure. Meanwhile, success becomes a double jeopardy: Success creates expectations which in turn increase the disappointment of eventual failure. Success also makes it difficult to excuse yourself from taking care of yourself and others. The more successful you are, the more difficult it is to pretend you haven't got what it takes to take full charge of yourself and your life.

A young woman with an eating disorder recalled that she had been doing well for a year and was about to graduate as an x-ray technician when she began her most severe episode of binges and vomiting. This episode culminated in a suicide attempt and subsequent hospitalization. She never completed her training.

The philosophy behind these traps is: *Better dissatisfied, pessimistic and in control* (or numbed by drugs, alcohol, food or workaholism) *than optimistic, uncertain and frightened.* Pessimism is the coward's escape. And cynicism often is the way out used by bright pessimists. The credo of those who fall into *The Fear of Failure and Success Traps* is: "Since life has no guarantees and can be extremely painful, I'd rather be dissatisfied and in control by expecting the worst and settling for what I have than try for well-being. If I tried my best and failed I would prove my worst fears are accurate—that I *am* worthless."

People caught in *The "There's No Use Trying" Trap* cry out for God or fate to come to the rescue. They may wait forever. Anyone can choose hopelessness, inaction or half-hearted efforts instead of trying wholeheartedly and risking the unknown. But time is always running out. Why waste unexplored and undeveloped talents?

There are two kinds of failure: cowardly failure and courageous failure. *Cowardly failure* is to fail without a good try. *Courageous failure* is to fail despite your best efforts. To try enthusiastically and fail is disappointing. But at least trying wholeheartedly guarantees self-respect and offers you the only chance you have at feeling fulfilled.

Success and failure have nothing to do with a person's worth. If you associate success and failure with your sense of worth, self-respect and fulfillment are impossible. Even smashing success is not fulfilling if it is achieved without really trying. Success alone can never give you a sense of worth.

What if nothing in the universe is either good or bad and there is no ultimate goal or point or meaning to life other than the one each of us chooses for ourselves? Maybe everything—past, present and future—is simply happening, and the best you can do is to feel good about yourself and how you behave. Perhaps Grantland Rice was right when he said the important thing is how you play the game. Maybe success and failure are secondary.

A New Direction

Accept that your worth is not an issue, but your self-respect is. You can earn self-respect by enthusiastically trying to discover, refine and use what is within you. Life without self-respect is empty. Fortunately, you can earn self-respect any time you are willing to face your fears. *Self-respect is the only thing in life entirely within your control.* Why not make life an exciting adventure of discovery guided by self-respect? Why not make self-respect the "bottom line" goal of life, and success the bonus?

Work on adopting the following perspective:

Of course I'd like to achieve my goals. But I know I'll only find fulfillment in success achieved through self-respecting efforts. Success without self-respect would feel empty.

If I fail despite my best efforts, I'll still benefit. Courageous failure lets me know when it's time to shift to potentially more fulfilling pursuits. No matter how long it takes to become successful or how many different things I have to try, at least I'll have my self-respect along the way.

I'd rather try my best, feel afraid and be proud of myself than just plod along. Right now it's less important *what* I try than *how hard* I try. I need to do something with all my heart. I need to taste the pride, excitement and fear that comes from giving all I've got.

Chapter 14

The Blame Trap

"People will allow their faults to be shown them; they will let themselves be punished for them; they will patiently endure many things because of them; they only become impatient when they have to lay them aside.

Goethe

"I Blame Myself":

"I keep screwing up and ruining everything. There must be something wrong with me."

"One of man's greatest failings is that he looks almost always for an excuse in the misfortune that befalls him through his own fault, before looking for a remedy—which means he often finds the remedy too late."

Cardinal de Retz

"I Blame Others (or Fate or God)":

"My difficulties aren't my fault."

Commonly Associated Features

People in *The Blame Trap* may have the following characteristics:

- tendency to criticize and blame themselves and others
- need to be in control and right, or at least not wrong
- difficulty accepting comforting
- tendency to be opinionated and defensive
- easily upset by criticism

Climbing Out of the Rut

Liz and Alan had been married for fifteen years. They had three children. Liz was a violinist with the local symphony. Alan was a hardworking corporate executive. Liz dragged Alan in to consult with me about their marriage.

Liz and Alan's complaints weren't unusual. Liz admitted that Alan was devoted to her. He often bought her gifts and frequently told her he loved her. But these things just weren't enough. She said Alan spent all his time working, watching television and going deep-sea fishing. She complained that he never revealed his true feelings and wasn't concerned about what *she* thought or felt except when he wanted her to applaud his accomplishments or commiserate with him about his problems at work. Liz said Alan resented her and became irritated whenever she was unhappy.

Alan compared Liz to his mother, "a martyr who needs to control everyone and always be the center of attention." Alan complained that Liz had never been physically affectionate except during their brief courtship. She seemed to have no appreciation for his work and the freedom and comforts his sizable income provided, comforts which she obviously enjoyed but took for granted.

Both agreed their sex life had always been a disappointment. And both privately boasted that their satisfying extramarital experiences "proved" their unsatisfactory sex together was the other's problem.

Liz and Alan would come in to see me whenever a crisis developed in their relationship. They were always ready to accuse each other but never prepared to take a close look at themselves and experiment with more compassionate and respectful attitudes.

Liz and Alan weren't happy. They didn't respect themselves and they hated the bickering and deceit in their marriage. Both were worried about how the children would be affected by the negative atmosphere in their home. But they were stuck in their familiar rut, pointing fingers and blaming each other.

Liz understood that she had to change how she treated Alan if she wanted him to change. But, despite increasing unhappiness, she couldn't bring herself to use a strategy which she agreed had a chance of improving their situation: Give Alan warmth and understanding and let him know that if her kindness and compassion were not eventually reciprocated, she would have to find loving support elsewhere and leave him.

Instead of adopting this positive approach to get what she wanted and perhaps save their marriage, Liz withheld her tenderness and support from Alan, and became involved with Don, a younger man who was gentle, warm and open. Liz continued to pounce on Alan with any evidence that confirmed her expectations of maltreatment and justified her resentment of him.

Liz used blame and an affair to avoid facing self-change. She was afraid to be on her own so she stayed with Alan. After all, Alan was a good provider, the children loved him and he was generous.

Why were Liz and Alan so resentful of one another, although they had been loving during their courtship and with their current lovers? Because a lover is a challenge, a person to be won over in order to reassure oneself about one's worth. The lover is a romantic *outsider* whose love can be accepted during the temporary insanity and lust of courtship. Once an outsider becomes family, ghosts from one's original family come alive to haunt a relationship. Set up housekeeping with a legitimate partner and unhealthy patterns from one's childhood family will reemerge and begin to interfere with respect and caring.

Alan and Liz could intellectually appreciate that they both felt the same kind of pain, rejection and loneliness around one another that they had experienced during childhood around their original families. Their self-doubt and negative expectations of each other made it impossible for either of them to accept love that was offered by someone they regarded as family. Yet they needed someone to depend on, someone to reassure them and compensate for their self-doubt. Both were terrified to be alone to face the emptiness and inadequacy they felt.

Despite their hunger for love and understanding, Alan and Liz also needed each other to be just as they were, because each reaffirmed the other's familiar and flawed sense of self. It was easier to have affairs and blame each other for their discontent than to look inside themselves and try to change.

Eventually, with loving, understanding and support from Don, some counseling and a great deal of courage, Liz stopped worrying about whether she was good enough. (On accepting one's worth, see Chapter 4, *The Self-Doubt Trap: Escape Route*, pp. 42–48.) Liz decided to live alone with her children for awhile to get to know and trust herself. With time and practice, when Alan or the grandparents were taking care of the children, Liz was also able to enjoy some solitude. She had always gone out of her way to take care of her children, friends, Alan, her lover and anyone else around her who needed help. Now she began to stand up for herself and say "no" sometimes in order to care for her own spirit. Liz was excited and proud of her increasing self-respect and self-reliance, but occasionally she had to endure feeling anxious and lonely.

I never saw Alan again after he and Liz separated. I hope he has grown as much as Liz. Unfortunately, men find it harder to seek help in order to better understand and care for themselves. Instead, many recently divorced or widowed men find and settle down with a new woman they hope will take care of them.

Liz was fortunate—she was in her thirties, had a devoted lover, and was established in her own career. Middle-aged women, women with children or those without work experience often feel devastated when they find themselves divorced or widowed, especially if they lack compassion and respect for themselves.

Pointing the Finger

Blame is so pervasive no single example can do it justice. Arthur and Doris of *The "People Don't Change" Traps* (pp. 118−121) and Ron and Barbara of *The "My Happiness is Your Responsibility" Traps* (pp. 151−153) are other examples of couples treating each other as scapegoats rather than as supportive partners.

Relationships are rich soil for the cultivation of blame. Blame, with its long and venerable tradition, has deep roots and a widespread influence in our culture. Society not only condones blame but encourages it.

Parents blame the bad influence of other children for the unsavory actions of their own offspring. Therapists blame therapy failures on their clients' lack of motivation. Divorce attorneys make their living capitalizing on the animosity and blame-seeking of estranged spouses. Children and experts blame parents, especially mothers, for all kinds of problems. Politicans blame anyone and everyone—from other countries to one another and, if all else fails, loyal sycophants on their own staff—in order to avoid accountability for their actions.

A major wellspring for blame in our society is the legal system. Our legal system proceeds as if money alone were sufficient to compensate for all forms of damage. The legal credo is: "If something bad happens, someone is to blame and should pay." This tradition supports millions of people—judges, attorneys, court reporters, clerks, psychiatrists and other experts—but it discourages personal responsibility.

Blame flourishes in the painful circumstances surrounding the unexpected deaths of young children whether from sudden crib death or from other causes such as acute leukemia. Couples who have little experience with comforting or being comforted are especially susceptible to blame. Many marriages never recover from the tragic loss of a child. Fortunately, support groups have been organized nationally that encourage couples to adopt compassionate attitudes towards their pain and grief. These self-help groups can help reduce the blame, resentment and loneliness which grow in the absence of comforting.[1]

In addition to blaming others and being blamed by others, people blame themselves for their dissatisfaction instead of pursuing more constructive alternatives. Sy, the client discussed in the previous chapter, is an example of someone who gets in his own way by blaming himself.

Escape Route
Exposing the Trap

Feeling blame when someone is hurt is human and understandable. *Getting stuck* in blame is a destructive waste of time and energy.

---

[1]*Compassionate Friends is one such group; Sudden Infant Death Foundation is another.*

When things go wrong and people get hurt, blame is the channel of least resistance for release of frustration and anger. It is much easier to blame a scapegoat than to examine and change oneself or society.

If the rush to blame were merely a search to determine who is responsible in order to correct a situation and prevent its reoccurence, blame would be far less destructive than it is. But, in practice, blame goes far beyond attribution of responsibility. Blame includes criticism and disapproval of the blameworthy person along with a desire to punish.

Blame is a poor substitute for comforting and constructive action. It is the poison created by uncomforted hurt. Blaming siphons attention and energy away from constructive change. Nothing is solved by blame. Bad situations are only aggravated. Consider the cycle of blame:

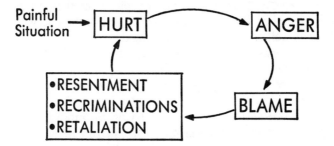

What are the consequences of this blame sequence? For dissatisfied, uncomforted and self-doubting people, *The Blame Trap* provides a crutch to cope with hurt, fear of defectiveness and reluctance to take responsibility for their own well-being. Blame distracts them from having to face a situation and make the best of it.

Without realizing it, people in *The Blame Trap* are saying:

I'm in pain. I feel awkward receiving comforting. If I blame my bad feelings on someone else, then I'm not responsible and won't have to face my fear of being flawed. If I can blame someone else, I can pretend that takes care of the problem. Then I don't have to take charge of my own well-being and do what I can to make myself feel better.

Like the other *Fear of Responsibility and Failure Traps,* blame lets you avoid trying. Preoccupation with blame can also be used to avoid facing pain. For example, many families use blame, anger and law suits to evade the full burden of grieving the death of a loved one.

Blame allows you to live in the past instead of doing your best in the present to create a better future. Because blame focuses on the past, by repeatedly concentrating attention on the offenses and injuries, blame perpetuates the unfortunate situation it is supposed to correct.

The blame sequence alienates people from themselves and one another. Blame is toxic to the spirit of the one who blames as well as the one who is blamed.

Blaming *oneself* is an insidiously clever deception. If you blame yourself you are unconsciously using a subtle maneuver to escape responsibility for your well-being. It appears as if you are willing to shoulder complete responsibility, yet really you are shirking the risk of trying to improve your situation. If you blame yourself you can run away from doing what you know would earn you self-respect. As long as you keep putting yourself down you don't have to try to change. Self-blame isn't a step in the direction of consructive action. It's just another way to reinforce your familiar pessimistic view of yourself and the world.

Blaming yourself for unsatisfying results even when you have put forth your best efforts means you have a cold and unforgiving materialistic attitude. Believing "success is everything" is unfair to yourself. It denies realistic limitations. No one is in complete control of results. A bottom-line orientation appears practical and responsible, but it indicates an unwillingness to make self-respect your highest priority in life. Believing success is *the* answer betrays severe self-doubt and the need to prove your worth by accomplishment.

Blame is *never* constructive. It is always a detour away from compassion, self-respect and self-acceptance. Divorce without personal change is never sufficient for well-being. Blaming others doesn't earn a politician the public's trust. Financial compensation for damages can never take the place of self-acceptance, comforting for pain or self-respect for enthusiastic efforts. Offering compassion and doing something positive to improve a situation are infinitely more productive ways to cope when something goes wrong.

A New Direction

Blaming is easier than taking the initiative to overcome difficulties. Perhaps you get stuck in blame because you're not accustomed to grieving and being comforted when you're suffering.

Why not change your attitude about blame? Regardless of who may be held responsible for your difficulties, why not save the energy wasted in anger, blame and resentment? You can *refuse* to agonize in blame. Assigning blame won't help you in any way except to indulge my self-righteousness. Instead of falling into the blame-as-an-answer cycle (page 145), you can view blame as a message:

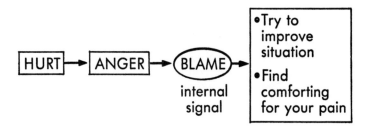

See if the following attitude helps:

I need to treat my feelings of blame as a message from my spirit that I feel hurt, need comforting and should do something to increase my self-respect and improve my situation.

The next time I feel like blaming someone, I'm going to write down how I've been hurt and some specific things I can do to feel better. Then, instead of aggravating my pain by getting caught up in anger and resentment, I'm going to begin doing the things I've written down and get some comforting.

CHAPTER 15

The "My Happiness is Your Responsibility" Traps

**"Who
Cannot resolve upon a moment's notice
To live his own life, he forever lives
A slave to others."**

Gotthold Ephraim Lessing

The Dependency Trap:

"I have to rely on someone else to make decisions. I can't trust my own thoughts, feelings and judgments."

The "Love Me And Make Me Whole" Trap:

"If no one is committed to me, it must mean something is wrong with me. Everything would be fine if only someone would give me the love I've always wanted but never had."

The Complacent Partner Trap:

"Now that I've got someone, I can take him or her for granted. I no longer have to take care of myself."

The Searching for the Perfect Love Trap:

"No one I've met is good enough. I'll just keep looking for someone who'll give me the love I need to make me feel whole "

Commonly Associated Features

People in *The "My Happiness Is Your Responsibility" Traps* may have some of the following characteristics:

- difficulty making decisions and dependent on the opinions of others
- reluctance to take on new responsibilities or try new things
- reluctance to expose true feelings
- anxiety when things are going well
- easily upset by criticism
- tendency to be critical and blaming of themselves
- difficulty accepting honest praise
- tendency to avoid confrontations at almost any cost

Four Out of Five People Surveyed . . .

Barbara met Ron at work. He was her supervisor and had hired her. Barbara admired him from the beginning. Ron was good at his job and confident in his abilities. Within a couple of months they were dating.

The woman Ron had lived with for two years left him for another man. Ron was still licking his wounds when he met Barbara. Barbara felt sorry for Ron and he appreciated her support. She began spending more and more nights at his place and, at his urging, decided to move in with him.

Ron's jealousy and possessiveness were understandable to Barbara, considering the rejection he had just suffered. But soon after they began living together, Barbara found herself being interrogated and even angrily accused of infidelity when she candidly told him of coffee or lunches with old friends.

Despite several ugly scenes, they were married within a year. All of this occurred twelve years before their first session with me. Barbara came to see me after an episode in which Ron struck her in front of the children.

Barbara endured Ron's angry moods—his sullen withdrawal into silence for hours or even days and his explosive outbursts—because she knew he was devoted to her. He worked hard, made a decent living, didn't drink or have any interest in other women. Besides, his jealousy and need to control was a continual reminder of how important she was to him.

Barbara's parents had demonstrated loving concern for their children by establishing clear rules and strict discipline and by actively participating in every decision affecting their children's lives, from school to friendships.

Barbara was a popular teenager but was more of a follower than a leader. Barbara relied on her friends' advice to make decisions. She ran her life as if conducting a Gallup poll. Although Ron's escalation from private intimidation to striking her in front of the children had upset her tremendously, Barbara didn't seek help until her best friend insisted. Even then, Barbara only agreed on the condition that her friend accompany her to the first session.

When I explored Barbara's goals for our consultation, I discovered she hoped I might convince her husband to be kinder. Barbara was terrified to stand up to Ron. She was afraid he would get angry and decide to leave her. When I suggested that Ron might be at least as frightened of losing *her*, Barbara was pleased but doubtful. Despite Ron's severe reaction to losing his previous relationship and his clinging attachment to her, Barbara couldn't believe she could get Ron to treat her and the children with respect and consideration.

Many people are like Barbara. They ask everyone they know—from their friends to their therapists, from Ann Landers to their hairdressers—what they should do. Either they allow someone else to take over or they procrastinate until situations get resolved by default. By letting someone else make their decisions, they avoid responsibility for what happens. If things work out to their satisfaction, their dependency is reinforced. If things turn out badly, they can blame someone else.

In men like Ron dependency is less obvious. Dependent men often function well outside the home but lack initiative and responsibility around their wives, especially if their wives are competent caretakers. Once they settle down with a woman, these men become more like the oldest child in the home than a competent and supportive partner.

However, when it comes to sex, dependent, controlling men are no different from most others. They need their partners' enthusiastic sexual response to be reassured that they are loved. But most women find that sexual desire and respect for a man go hand-in-hand. If a man is consistently passive and dependent on a woman, she usually becomes resentful and her respect and romantic feelings for him dwindle.

Of course, women can also become childish and dependent once they settle into a relationship. Sometimes women (and men) marry to avoid financial and personal responsibility. Taking care of oneself and one's own spirit is life's most demanding challenge, frequently abdicated to anyone who seems willing to assume it.

Escape Route
Exposing the Trap

The *"My Happiness Is Your Responsibility" Traps* have in common the avoidance of responsibility for oneself and one's spirit. Giving up the responsibility of caring for yourself and your spirit is the antithesis of maturity. These Mind Traps are a direct result of self-doubt: "How can I rely on myself when I feel so defective?"

It is difficult to risk having faith, compassion and respect for yourself when no one else ever has. Yet there is no alternative if you want self-respect and well-being.

Your sense of what is right, refined by experience and common sense, is a unique and indispensable guidance system. Only if you conduct your life with guidance from your spirit can you lead a healthy, satisfying life.

People in *The "Love Me and Make Me Whole" Trap* and *The Searching for the Perfect Love Trap* are eternally searching for someone to make them feel better. They are frequently alone and lonely. People in these two traps reject anyone who is interested in them because of one flaw or another. They are searching for the person who will give them the unconditional love they never received. But the search is futile. Unconditional love isn't available in adulthood. And even if they were to find someone who offered them more than they had ever experienced, they would feel undeserving and be unable to accept it.

People in *The Dependency Trap* and *The Complacent Partner Trap* have abandoned themselves to someone else's care and given up responsibility for their own well-being. Satisfaction for any length of time is impossible in a dependent relationship. No one can take care of you as well as you can. No one else feels what you feel; no one else receives direct messages from your spirit indicating what you need and what will earn your self-respect.

Others are unlikely to make your well-being their highest priority for very long. And when others finally do let you down, you'll blame them without noticing that you set up the betrayal—you expected too much from them and abandoned yourself and your spirit long before they did.

Dependency is a bad bargain. Dependency trades self-determination and freedom for the false promises of security and safety. Except in acute crisis and severe disability, dependency is always associated with a loss of self-respect. Many people have lived to regret yielding responsibility for their lives to experts and leaders like psychiatrists, lawyers, financial managers and gurus. To consult is one thing; to obey is another. Dependency and irresponsibility are the basis of the blind obedience that make cults, mass movements and genocide possible.

People who are dependent because they are worried about being inherently defective can never receive enough love to be satisfied. Besides, what a dependent person gets isn't love in the sense of real and reciprocal caring. Often it is obligation and pity tainted with disrespect and resentment.

Dependent people often choose partners who habitually take responsibility for others—people who continually treat their companions like children. (See Chapter 23, *The "Your Happiness Is My Responsibility" Trap*, for more about people who take care of others' needs before their own.)

Insecurity is the bond in a dependent relationship. Low self-respect and resentment are warning signals of a relationship based on dependency.

A Dependency Check List

1. Do I resent the other person without telling them?

2. Am I afraid to live without this person?

3. Do I cover up and apologize for this person?

4. Have my friends hinted that I'm putting up with too much from this person?

5. Do I complain about this person to other people?

6. Do I keep nagging without taking a strong stand to do something about inconsiderate treatment?

A New Direction

No one else can make better decisions for your life than you can. You may not know for certain what's best for you, but rest assured that no one is in a better position to collect information and experiment to find out. Regardless of your limitations, you must accept responsibility for yourself.

Learn to take loving care of the injured and needy child inside who worries about being defective, instead of expecting someone else to do it. Before you can find and accept anyone else's love, you must become an understanding and comforting parent to that inner child. Have compassion for your pain, fears, mistakes and weaknesses. Everyone gets hurt and makes mistakes. *No one should have to suffer without comforting.*

Your greatest challenge is to put your spirit's well-being ahead of everything else, including concern about losing what you have. It's your responsibility to *make certain* you receive fair and respectful treatment from others. Constantly complaining to others and feeling sorry for yourself wastes time and damages your self-respect. The responsible adult part of you, however inexperienced it may be, must negotiate with others on behalf of the needy and vulnerable inner child.

No one owes you anything you haven't earned. You can't expect your partner to offer unconditional love. Only rare parents have unconditional love to offer. If your parents weren't able to give you as much nurturing and respect as you needed, you can't expect them to make it up to you.

You either received the care and nurturing you needed, or you didn't. If not, you must go through the awkward and difficult process of learning to have compassion and respect for yourself. It's too late for anyone else to take that kind of responsibility for your inner child.

Consider adopting the following attitude:

It's a waste of time and energy to blame anyone. I have to mourn what I wished I could have had during childhood and learn to settle for the best I can barter for from others, who have had their own disappointments and wounds. I have to ask for what I need and give what I can in return.

To master the art of living requires the courage to risk trial and error experimentation and occasional failures and embarrassment. The freedom and self-respect I'll earn from learning to depend on myself is worth the burden.

I want to be with people who take responsibility for their own well-being but will share life's joys and pain with me. They have to be people who make life better for me. To have a loving partnership, we both have to admit we have weaknesses and make mistakes. We need to be honest about how we feel. When we're hurt, we must be willing to give and accept comforting instead of being critical and defensive.

Caring about someone and enjoying the same in return isn't dependency. When I care about others, I feel warm and compassionate towards them; I rejoice when they're happy and am sad when they're hurt and unhappy. But I must have the same warm and compassionate attitude toward my own spirit, too.

If the people I care about are treating themselves, others or me with insufficient respect, I won't hesitate to stop them. If I can't get them to change, I'll refrain from associating with them *no matter how much I love them, even if they are family.* To do less is dependency and puts my need for a relationship ahead of loving concern for my spiritual well-being and for the well-being of the person I profess to love.

Dependency on others is not the same as the mutual support necessary for healthy partnerships, communities and the survival of the human race. I must review my current situation regularly to be certain I'm not betraying what in my heart I know is right for the sake of keeping a relationship or being a member of a group.

Stop *asking* people to make decisions for you. Start *telling* people your opinions and be willing to negotiate instead of always going along with what others want.

Make a list of specific things you could do to have more respect for yourself. Then go ahead and risk trying some of those things.

PART 7

The Fear of
Rejection Traps

CHAPTER 16

The Rejection Trap

"It seems that it is madder never to abandon one's self than often to be infatuated; better to be wounded, a captive and a slave, than always to walk in armor."

Margaret Fuller

"Less Intimacy, Less Pain":

"I can't trust you enough to get close. I'm afraid you'll end up leaving me and I'll be so hurt I won't be able to handle it. The less I open myself up to you, the better."

"The restraints we impose on ourselves to refrain from loving are often more cruel than the severities of our beloved."

La Rochenfoucald

"Better to Reject than Be Rejected":

"I'm so afraid I'll be rejected. I'd better get what I can from you and then find some excuse to reject you before I get too committed, vulnerable and hurt."

"I love you and, because I love you, I would sooner have you hate me for telling the truth than adore me for telling you lies."

Pietro Aretino

Control the News:

"I'm afraid no one would care about me if they knew what I really thought and felt. I don't want to burden you, hurt you or lose you, so I'd better only reveal what won't upset you."

Commonly Associated Features

People in *The Rejection Trap* may have the following characteristics:

- reluctance to expose true feelings

- easily upset by criticism

- need to impress others with their accomplishments or appearance

- tendency to be jealous

- difficulty asking for or accepting comforting

- addictions to harmful people, substances or habits

Behind the Mask

Dana was in her early thirties. A well-dressed sales executive, she came across as confident and disarmingly assertive. But this slick, polished veneer was merely the mask she wore at work. Dana was an insecure person in disguise.

Dana's self-assured act was maintained at great cost. Her performance exhausted her emotionally and physically.

Most evenings when she didn't have to work, Dana collapsed in front of the TV, too drained to socialize and too tired even to read. The rewards she harvested from her work (money, prestige, influence, praise and a sense of purpose) left her dissatisfied. Dana felt her achievements were the result of hypocrisy, a deliberately maintained posture calculated to impress others and hide her weaknesses.

Dana's work was the only fulfilling aspect of her life. She was an example of that common paradox—a highly talented, successful, admired and yet lonely person. Although Dana knew a couple of women she considered close friends, there were many things about herself she wouldn't tell them because she feared their disapproval.

The reason she consulted me was the disappointing pattern of her relationships with men. Dana had been married eight years and divorced for three when she came to see me. She had met her husband, Jim, at college. Both were conventional people who conformed to what was expected. What had begun as mild infatuation evolved into a comfortable arrangement. Eventually marriage seemed like the intelligent thing to do. But Dana and Jim never managed to become true friends and whatever passion they had felt at first rapidly dissipated.

Dana and Jim eventually began to quarrel about Jim's poorly concealed infidelities. Dana bitterly demanded that Jim pay more attention to her, their sons and their home. After years of fighting, they agreed to divorce.

Shortly after the divorce, Dana found a job selling insurance. She threw herself into her work with phenomenal results. Within a year she became the local office's top salesperson. Within two, she became sales manager.

As a queen bee in a predominantly male business, Dana had no trouble finding dates. After a date Dana would wait impatiently for the man to call back. If he didn't call immediately, Dana would become frantic, call her friends, explain what she and the man had said and done on the date and then beg for reassurance and advice about what tactics she could use to keep the man interested in her.

To impress Dana, a man had to come across as strong— he had to be successful, aloof and confident. She said that men who were "too mushy and fell in love right off the bat" were boring and made her uncomfortable. The more hard-to-get he seemed, the more obsessed she became.

Dana found it almost impossible to be assertive in her personal relationships with men. The more she admired a man, the more careful and awkward she was around him and the less she revealed about herself to avoid scaring him off.

Dana had difficulty maintaining the interest of any man she was attracted to. And any man who didn't want her confirmed her worst fears about herself. To Dana, rejection meant she wasn't good enough.

In response to my questioning, Dana admitted that several men candidly explained their disappointment in her. They had been attracted by her intelligence, her flashes of dry wit when discussing business, her physical appearance and her apparent competence and independence. But she quickly lost her appeal away from the professional arena. On dates she became boring, wishy-washy and insecure. One moment she would be a dependent little girl, the next a smothering, overprotective mother.

Dana admitted that away from work she allowed men to take her for granted and treat her with disrespect. Her desperate need to maintain a man's interest had little to do with how much she admired the man or how warmly she felt towards him. She just could not stand to be rejected by *any* man. She made sure I understood her severe panic about feeling unwanted.

After getting hurt, Dana would retreat into a hermit-like existence. She would swear off men, become standoffish and refuse to date. Loneliness was easier to bear than the pain of rejection. It was safer to resign herself to a life of work and to friendships with women who were more accepting.

Dana saw herself as an imposter. She believed she was overrated and had fooled everyone at work. The charade exhausted her. Being around anyone was a strain. She felt constantly on guard, yet being alone didn't offer complete relief either. She needed to be distracted from her private thoughts and feelings by food, television or work.

Dana thought she had been extremely fortunate in having come from such a good and happy family. The oldest of four, Dana had helped her working mother with household chores and supervision of her siblings. She admitted some resentment of this role but felt guilty about being so selfish. No one in their family ever argued. Their home was a peaceful, orderly place where people didn't upset one another.

Dana became irritated and defensive when I pressed her for details: Were her parents physically demonstrative of their love? Was there comforting for emotional distress? Did they get support and understanding from each other when they were upset?

Gradually Dana revealed her childhood from another perspective. The calm atmosphere of her home had been maintained at a price. High standards were implicit. No one burdened anyone else with problems. Everyone in the family tried to please everyone else no matter what they really thought or felt. Dana said her parents were so devoted to each other and the children she couldn't stand upsetting them.

Behavior considered inappropriate was discussed among the family with a tone of sadness and charitable concern. In this way, her parents' expectations were made clear without need for definite rules or strong sanctions.

I had Dana bring in childhood photographs. In each picture she was crisp and sanitized—no messiness, silliness, laughter or physical contact.

Dana could see how she had learned to believe she could be loved only if she were pleasing. This was not her parents deliberate purpose, only an unfortunate consequence of their best intentions. Her father was rarely at home and was never physically demonstrative. Occasionally he'd show his love for his daughters by leaving little presents on their beds, winking at them privately or gently teasing them. Dana couldn't bear the thought of threatening her delicate but precious bond with her father by disappointing him in any way, even after he began to favor each of her younger sisters in succession. Dana's mother was always concerned and protective of Dana, continually educating her about what would help her be successful in a world that, like it or not, was dominated by men.

Was it any wonder, I asked Dana, that she was uncomfortable with adoring men and attracted to those who were emotionally aloof? Wasn't that reminiscent of her relationship with her father? Wasn't her mother's relationship with Dana's father a dependent and ingratiating one? Didn't her mother give Dana the message that finding a man and holding onto him was the very definition of success in a woman's life? How could Dana be adept at understanding her feelings and accepting comforting when she had been brought up to hide what she felt?

No one was to blame. But if Dana was ever to accept herself and stop humiliating herself around men she admired, she would have to recognize and accept the lonely little girl within her who needed tenderness and support.

Changing has been a struggle for Dana. She has had to increase her awareness of her feelings and develop a more compassionate attitude towards her pain and her needs. Making self-respect more important than pleasing men has required her to alter her perspective. She has had to see her hurt as the plea from her wounded inner child instead of evidence she is defective.

In order to change, Dana has had to risk confronting men

who take her for granted. She has done everything from awkwardly and tearfully explaining her feelings in person to writing carefully composed letters. She has had to rehearse alone and in front of friends to state her point of view without justifying her feelings or blaming a man for feeling what he feels. But Dana had the advantage of an excellent role model close at hand: She emulated the way she handles herself with men in her professional life, where she is a charming woman and, at the same time, a smart, tough and fair negotiator.

Escape Route
Exposing the Trap

If you doubt yourself, the pain of rejection feels like proof of your worthlessness. *The Fear of Rejection Traps* (*The Rejection Traps, The Jealousy Trap* and *The Shy and Lonely Traps*) are attempts to avoid intimacy in order to sidestep the full impact of rejection. But to continuously be on guard against rejection wastes energy that could be spent on constructive attitudes and actions.

Like death, rejection and failure can happen at anytime, whether or not you live in constant fear of them. With self-doubt, the stakes get higher: your fundamental worth is at risk in every situation. To be afraid of death, loss, rejection and failure is natural. But to equate rejection and failure with being defective is wrong. No one is defective. Rejection *is painful* but says nothing about *self-worth.*

Self-doubt exaggerates the importance you give to how others feel about you. Because of insecurity, you *need* others to like you not only to avoid loneliness but *to avoid feeling worthless.* The irony of self-doubt is that you can't accept and rejoice in another person's love or admiration if you feel flawed and undeserving.

Like Sisyphus eternally pushing his stone up the hill but doomed to never reach the crest, if you have self-doubt you struggle to win people over but can never accept their love and admiration. As a result, you end up losing interest in anyone who wants you.

Although being rejected says nothing about your inherent worth, repeated rejections may say something about how you've been treating others, about the kind of people you've chosen and about what you tolerate from others. If you are regularly rejected, you may have one or more of the following characteristics:

1. You may repeatedly select partners who are ungiving or unpredictable, people who are a challenge to win over, who evoke feelings reminiscent of your emotionally dissatisfying childhood.

2. Others may regard you as aloof and even rejecting because of your shyness or conceit.

3. You may tolerate disrespect from others.

These three attitudes dramatically increase the likelihood of rejection. They result from the childhood experiences that create self-doubt.

Developing and sustaining a good relationship is a difficult process, even when the people involved have self-acceptance. A satisfying relationship is unlikely if you look to it for reassurance about your worth. Relationships can't prove you're worthwhile.

No one was put on earth to pass judgement on another's value as a human being. Self-worth is simply too valuable an egg to risk entrusting to anyone else's basket. Your worth is yours as soon as you can find the courage to accept it on faith.

If you shun close relationships because the risk of rejection is too high, isolation and loneliness are inevitable.

Avoiding intimacy is terribly expensive insurance against the pain of loss.

The art of living well necessitates taking risks to increase your chances of finding intimacy. Aren't you better off occasionally hurt by rejection but confident in your worth and compassionate enough to arrange comforting for your pain, instead of avoiding closeness, feeling chronically lonely and being filled with self-doubt?

Control the News (see page 162) is a specific tactic people use to avoid rejection. Controlling the news makes intimacy impossible. Any tenderness and comfort offered to people who control the news is tainted by their realization that they have not been honest. As a result of hiding some important thoughts, they can't accept the caring they receive. People in this trap are always concerned: "How would the other person feel if they knew how I really think and feel?"

By hiding what you fear would offend others, you end up inhibiting spontaneity, honesty and openness. If you suppress your hurt and anger, your resentment will grow and you'll become emotionally distant. Hiding your feelings poisons a relationship and increases the likelihood of rejection.

If you don't reveal what you truly feel you can create the *appearance* of a good relationship. But if you misrepresent yourself, you'll never really feel cared for and understood. Your inner child will continue to be as lonely and deprived as it was in childhood.

Control the News is part of the overprotection racket practiced by families who don't know how to comfort one another. Parents hide painful frightening facts from their children; children, in turn, learn to protect their parents and then carry this attitude into their adult relationships and the parenting of their own children.

Unfortunately, many people settle for superficial dishonest relationships instead of risking rejection. *Intimacy is as rare as the honesty and courage required to produce it*

A New Direction

Resolve not to blame yourself for your pain and fear. Fear of being hurt is unavoidable and human. Stop questioning your worth and begin to see pain as a signal sent by your troubled spirit. The pain you feel when you are criticized or rejected is evidence of how much you need to feel understood and accepted.

Instead of giving in to fear, view pain as an opportunity to rediscover and take loving responsibility for your wounded inner child. It's up to you to help this frightened part of you get the understanding, companionship and comforting it needs from other people, no matter how awkward it feels to ask for and accept.

Adopt the following attitude:

I have to realize that the child in me has been waiting a long time to get the understanding and comforting it needs. My loneliness and hurt aren't evidence that I'm defective. My pain can give me courage to reach out for closeness. I can earn self-respect by confronting my fear of rejection and becoming more open and loving.

The more wounded I felt and the less comforting and respect I received as a child, the more self-doubt I have and the more courage it will take to reach out. But I'm not alone. No one is immune. Everyone has to deal with the fear of rejection.

I need to find someone who is willing to be as considerate about my sensitivity as I would be in return. Anyone worth caring about will be understanding and patient if I explain what has caused me to be so afraid of being hurt.

If the person I'm with now is unwilling to work

together to increase the tenderness and respect we have for each other, I'll have to find enough self-respect and compassion for my spirit to face my fears and find someone else—someone willing to accept the fairest and most promising of relationship bargains: Do unto others as you would have them do unto you *and accept nothing·less in return.*

Inspiration from others can help. Getting involved with a group of people who have similar interests or struggles may also help you get over your fear of rejection.

Whether you join a new group of people or turn to those you already know, resolve to be more open about what you need from others.

If you're easily hurt, admit that to yourself. Your openness won't make you any more vulnerable than you already are, but it will increase your chances of getting what you need. Those who would misuse your openness against you are the kind of people you need to avoid from now on.

CHAPTER 17

The Jealousy Trap

"Love does not cause suffering: what causes
it is the sense of ownership, which is love's
opposite."

Saint-Exupery

The Jealousy Trap:

"I'm afraid you'll leave me for someone else. I want to
know everything you do while you're away from me. My
jealousy proves how much I love you."

Commonly Associated Features

People in *The Jealousy Trap* may have the following
characteristics:

- frequently envious and jealous
- difficulty asking for or accepting comforting
- pessimistic and cynical
- tendency to blame oneself
- easily upset by criticism
- promiscuous, at least in their fantasies

Once Burned, Twice Shy

Dan consulted me at Janine's insistence. Dan had difficulty trusting Janine. They had been dating for three years and considered themselves engaged, although there hadn't been an explicit marriage proposal. They spent most of their free time together, either at her home or his apartment. Yet Dan was tortured with fear and jealousy when they were separated for even one night.

Dan described his feelings to me:

Janine accuses me of not trusting her and watching her every move. I do call her when we're apart, but just to reassure myself. She is such a desirable woman and so friendly to everyone, I keep imagining her with other men. I know it seems ridiculous, but there's a part of me that *wants* to find her cheating on me, even though I'd be devastated. At least I'd know the worst for certain and I wouldn't have to keep waiting for it to happen.

Janine is ready to get married, but I'm afraid to because I'm not sure I can trust her. I went out on my wife a few times when I was married, but only after I found out that she had frequently been unfaithful to me. Our divorce was a horrible experience. I don't ever want to go through anything like that again.

She says I'm suffocating her and driving her crazy with my jealousy. If I don't get over this and agree to set a wedding date soon she's going to get fed up. She only has a few years left to have children and if it's not going to be with me, she'll have to find someone else. She's been so damn choosy up to now—in her thirties and never married—I keep wondering why she chose me. Maybe she's getting desperate . . . No, I'm just kidding [Dan added with an unconvincing smile].

Marlene is another example of someone caught in *The Jealousy Trap*. Marlene was obsessed with the conviction that her husband Steve was "fooling around all the time." She saw evidence of it everywhere. She would catch him looking at attractive women in restaurants, at parties, or while the two of them were driving or walking together. She saw proof of his infidelity in his changing moods, the timing of his showers and in his choice of clothes for the day.

"I'm a living, breathing man of reproductive age," Steve said, "How can I help *noticing* a good-looking woman?!" But he swore he had no interest in anyone else. Marlene's accusations were especially frustrating to Steve because he felt shy and awkward around women. Steve explained that both Marlene and his first wife had taken the initiative to meet him. "Compared to most men, I've had relatively little romantic and sexual experience. And I have absolutely no interest in having an affair."

Marlene complained bitterly about Steve's inattentiveness to her. In rebuttal Steve poured out evidence of his love—he often bought her gifts, they went on vacations together, he regularly complimented her on her intelligence and beauty, and he was always ready to have sex.

Marlene granted that all this was true. But she interpreted Steve's actions as superficial, unconvincing gestures. Depending on her mood, she could appreciate the gifts and vacations or see them as guilty attempts to buy her off. His compliments might be honestly intended, but, after all, he was a sucker for any woman with a pretty face and a well-rounded body. And she saw Steve's insatiable appetite for sex with her as evidence of where his (and every other man's) mind was located. Marlene's father had run off with another woman when Marlene was seven and she believed Steve would eventually do the same.

I asked Marlene, "What would convince you that Steve loves you and is devoted to you?" Embarrassed by what her answer implied, Marlene responded that she wasn't certain anything could convince her. But she argued that greater consideration and understanding of her feelings might help:

> He criticizes me for being upset. He expects me to support him no matter what, but can only stand to be around me when I'm happy. That's why he wants other women. Affairs are an easy escape into fantasy land— an ice cream sundae. Men are such selfish babies.

Steve protested:

> She wants me to listen and be understanding while she attacks me. I'm only human, So I get angry and defend myself. Who wouldn't? Dammit, I've never cheated on her. Sure I've had some fantasies, but I'll bet she's had a few herself. I may not be one of those wimpy European movie actor lovers she's always dreaming about, but I do love her and I show it every way I know. Someday I'll get fed up and stop trying to prove I love her. But you know what really bothers me? She'd just say, "I told you so!"

Escape Route
Exposing the Trap

The Jealousy Trap is an attempt to protect yourself against rejection which would confirm that there is something wrong with you. When you feel inadequate, no partner can be trusted. If you regard any partner as untrustworthy, being rejected can never be your fault. This pessimistic attitude allows you to blame rejection on the other person's deceitful nature instead of your own inadequacies.

The Jealousy Trap is an exorbitantly expensive insurance

policy against the pain of rejection. It provides no protection and actually increases the risk of rejection. A person caught in *The Jealousy Trap* is so preoccupied with guarding against rejection through possessiveness and suspicion that tenderness, openness and vulnerability become impossible. To be warm and trusting and then be betrayed would make you feel like a fool, or so it seems when you are insecure about your worth.

The misconception is that if you *anticipate* rejection it will hurt less than if it catches you by surprise. There is no truth to this belief. Rejection hurts just as much either way. Anticipating rejection merely increases the likelihood it will happen. Distrust and attempts to control ultimately provoke the very rejection that is feared.

Many people in *The Jealousy Trap* have a childhood history of parental infidelity or divorce, or felt neglected by their parents in some way. Victims of jealousy often unconsciously choose partners who treat them in ways that evoke familiar feelings of childhood rejection. Choosing such partners makes jealousy feel legitimate and rejection even more likely.

To get control of their jealousy, Dan and Marlene had to accept that their jealousy was their own responsibility and not their partner's. To have a better relationship with their partners, Dan and Marlene had to change their attitudes towards themselves. Although the *focus* of their fear and pain was *external* (their partners, Janine and Steve), they had to recognize that the *source* of their jealousy was *internal*. They had to examine the origins of their insecurity in their childhood experiences. Pain from inadequately comforted wounds had been preserved within them undiminished in intensity and had manifested itself in self-doubt and the fear of rejection.

Since Dan and Marlene doubted themselves, no one and nothing could reassure them for long. At least their jealousy gave them a feeling of control. Jealousy prepared them for the worst and helped shift their concerns from their own sense of inadequacy to the infidelity of their partners.

In order to change, Dan and Marlene had to consider new ways of looking at themselves. They had to take a chance and be more loving, more open and more vulnerable than they had risked since early childhood. Their partners cooperated by changing their attitudes too. Changing was awkward and frightening but nothing less could have saved their relationships and improved their lives.

A New Direction

Resolve to accept your feelings of jealousy and use them to help you change instead of letting yourself be controlled by them.

Jealousy reflects self-doubt and fear of rejection. Accept that jealousy is your responsibility to overcome. Shift your attention from your partner's actions to your feelings about yourself, whether or not your partner really is trustworthy.

Jealousy is evidence of having felt emotionally abandoned and hurt during childhood. If you can face and understand the childhood origins of your fears, you can develop compassion for your insecurities.

The following attitude will help:

I don't *blame* my parents, but I didn't receive as much comforting as I needed as a child. I didn't feel I could count on anyone to always care about me. As a result, I can't trust people who supposedly love me. I end up blaming them for not being able to be loving enough to convince me. Unfortunately, my distrust and attempts to control feel suffocating to others and drive them away.

If I want to save my relationship and avoid rejection, I need to explain the historical reasons for my jealousy to the person I care about. I have to admit it's my problem and my responsibility to handle. I also have to express my determination not to perpetuate jealousy by always trying to be in control. The less I act like a jealous person, the more rapidly my jealousy will fade, provided I keep working wholeheartedly to get rid of self-doubt.

When I *feel* jealous and frightened, I can use my jealous feelings as a signal that I feel hurt, lonely and afraid. Instead of *acting* jealous, I can learn to ask for loving reassurance from my partner.

When you feel jealous, try telling your partner:

I need your help. I'm feeling jealous. I need some reassurance that you love me and care about how I feel. A kind word or a hug from you would help me feel wanted.

You can act as if you're trusting despite your fear of being deceived and rejected. You'll earn your self-respect and your partner's appreciation if you find the courage to try this new attitude towards jealousy.

Your partner can assist you by keeping in mind that your jealousy reflects your insecurity and by refusing to become defensive and argumentative. Although defensive and angry reactions to being attacked are natural, they merely feed into your insecurities and aggravate your jealousy. Defensiveness feels like rejection not reassurance.

Instead of withdrawing or counterattacking, your partner can kindly but firmly reassure you that he or she loves you and wants to be with you but simply will not tolerate being interrogated, accused or controlled. Your partner can help immensely by offering as much tenderness and loving reassurance as possible, with the understanding that because you're not accustomed to warm and considerate treatment, you may not be able to accept it wholeheartedly at first.

The more trusting and loving you act, the more tenderness you will receive as a result. Eventually, you will feel less jealous, more loving and more loveable.

CHAPTER 18

The Shy and Lonely Trap

"Avoiding danger is no safer in the long run than outright exposure. The fearful are caught as often as the bold."

Helen Keller

Shyness:

"People can see right through me and can tell there's something wrong with me. The more I admire people, the more awkward I become. If I hide how I think and feel, others are less likely to discover my inadequacies."

"Man's loneliness is but his fear of life."

Eugene O'Neill

"Only Losers Are Lonely":

"I'm lonely. No one really cares about me. Other people have good friends and loving partners. There must be something wrong with me."

Commonly Associated Features

People in *The Shy and Lonely Trap* may have the following characteristics:

- tendency to avoid confrontations at any cost
- difficulty accepting comforting
- tendency to place other's needs and wishes ahead of their own
- fear of not being good enough
- easily upset by criticism
- tendency to show little enthusiam and avoid commitments
- difficulty accepting honest praise
- reluctance to expose true feelings
- tendency to be jealous

Life At Arm's Length

Ann was 31, single and overweight. She had only dated two men for any length of time. Henry, the first, was pleasant company but seemed too weak and dependent for Ann. He often expressed his love and desire to marry her. Ann ended up moving to California as a way of rejecting Henry's unrelenting proposals.

Sam, Ann's only other suitor, had given up on her just before she came to consult me. Apparently he was almost as quiet and retiring as Ann. They both enjoyed music and the theater. Neither felt the need to talk much, but they were comfortable together and occasionally would even become deeply involved in philosophical debates.

But Sam became frustrated with Ann's sexual inhibitions. His escalating dissatisfaction and Ann's refusal to see a counselor with him eventually made Sam decide to stop seeing her. When she realized Sam had really left her, Ann finally considered getting some help.

Ann felt she had to change the pattern of her life. She envied everyone around her for their freedom, spontaneity and network of friends. Ann desperately wanted to be "normal" and have a close and loving family, but she was losing hope that it would ever happen. She knew her shyness was a symptom of something deeper, although she didn't know what and was afraid nothing could be done about it.

Ann was a college graduate, an accomplishment which had required determined maneuvering in order to sidestep the school's public speaking requirement. She earned a modest living editing technical manuals. Her job bored her but she stuck with it because it involved little personal interaction with anyone other than two or three immediate colleagues. They seemed to like Ann and often invited her to join them for drinks or dinner after work. Usually she'd politely refuse, offering some lame excuse. Ann was convinced they felt sorry for her and were merely trying to be kind.

To describe Ann as sensitive and vulnerable would be an award-winning understatement. She could be hurt by almost anything, including the discomfort she perceived in those around her. She was considerate to a fault, always going out of her way to ensure that her wishes, her actions and even her mere presence did not inconvenience anyone. It was as if she wished to disturb as few molecules as possible.

Ann was retiring even around her large immediate family, with one notable exception: When young children were present—her younger brothers and sisters, her cousins, or even children she had never met—Ann would gravitate to them. She would immediately become the center of their attention, like a modern-day version of the Pied Piper. They would go off in a corner, read a book or play a game, and laugh and jabber away, as if insulated from the intimidating world of serious and critical adults.

Around her closest sister, Alexis, and Janet, her one real friend, Ann was witty and sometimes even hilariously outrageous. Her letters to them contained brilliant, incisive observations about mutual acquaintances. It was all but impossible for Alexis and Janet to honor their agreement with Ann to keep these letters absolutely confidential.

Ann's mother was a member of the unofficial sorority known as "supermoms." She handled and protected everyone around her at great sacrifice to her own needs, never revealing any discomfort or uttering the slightest complaint. Ann's father worked diligently as general manager of an appliance store and needed a peaceful retreat. So her mother made certain the family was on its best behavior whenever he was home.

Extremely shy since early childhood, Ann would burst into tears when merely asked an innocent question by a friendly stranger or teacher in school. Yet her timidity did not reflect passivity or inner calm. Although Ann tried hard to please and was rarely assertive, she could be stubborn and display a temper as severe as her father's when she felt relatively safe, especially when she was alone with her mother.

Her mother told me she'd sensed Ann's vulnerability from the beginning and had tried her best to protect Ann from becoming upset. Her father hated when anyone cried, especially if he felt there was nothing to cry about.

Recognizing Ann's talent as a writer, her mother tried to encourage her as much as possible. But she was puzzled by Ann's obviously low self-esteem. Everyone appreciated Ann's talent and would tell her so, yet their praise irritated Ann instead of pleasing her. (See Chapter 11, *The Biased Against Myself Traps*, regarding inability to accept compliments.)

I asked Ann, Alexis and their mother how feelings were handled in their family. If I had discovered that there had been a free flow of comforting, mutual understanding and physical affection, I would have retired from psychiatry in dismay.

In fact, Ann's father was a man of few words and often these words were so carefully selected, sharply honed and precisely aimed they could cut to the heart without noticeably interrupting the conversation. Her mother was exemplary in manifestly ignoring these criticisms, not betraying her feelings with even a ripple on the placid surface of her countenance. Disturbances were smoothed over as quickly as possible. Ann's mother deeply loved her family and was a world-class protector, but she was as unskilled as the rest of the family at comforting and at demonstrating affection with words, hugs or kisses.

Ann would often feel smothered by her mother's concern. All her life she had been treated as an invalid; she believed it and hated it. It was difficult for Ann to reconsider her negative sense of herself. It took a long time before she could expose her thoughts and feelings to anyone, even other women with similar problems in self-help groups. Every time Ann risked revealing something about herself, regardless of how supportive others were, she would panic, retreat and berate herself for her flaws. Ann was convinced that others were disappointed, critical and perhaps even disgusted by her self-disclosures. It took a long time before she could accept that she was projecting her negative feelings about herself onto others.

Ann's pain and feeling of defectiveness were such an integral part of her self-image that to reconsider her attitudes towards herself was extremely frightening. To accept herself, she had to abandon the only self she had ever known. The leap to self-acceptance would be colossal, given the severity of her self-doubt. She felt undeserving of the magic necessary for such a monumental transformation.

She began to revise her sense of herself only after she had been of help to many others with similar difficulties. Then, with a great deal of encouragement from her self-help group, Ann began to step back and consider being as fair and comforting to her own inner child as she was learning to be with others. Her experiments with self-acceptance required a tremendous amount of courage.

First Ann had to deliberately endure hurt, anxiety and anger as she started confronting her feelings about her family. To accept herself, she had to accept her hurt and anger.

Second, she had to put up with the awkwardness and hypocrisy she experienced when she tried to feel compassion for her bad feelings and when she began to reach out to others.

With practice and despite frequent retreats into self-deprecation and bashfulness, Ann finally could no longer reject her own spirit. Eventually, she was able to feel warmth for the hurt and frightened child in her. Along with this compassion came new faith in herself and her worth.

Escape Route
Exposing the Trap

Shyness reflects fear of criticism, humiliation and rejection for your thoughts, feelings and actions. If you're worried about being found defective, you'll be convinced you're the focus of everyone's attention and preoccupied with what everyone must be thinking about you. Because you're easily hurt, you'll be desperate to hide and protect yourself. But this keeps you lonely.

Most people are too busy with their own concerns to care about other people's weaknesses. Few people give a damn whether someone else has read the latest best seller or has cellulite-blemished thighs. Even if we allow that some people are intrigued by another person's weaknesses, at worst they are indulging in the misery-loves-company game, a pathetic attempt to reassure themselves because of their own sense of inadequacy. At best, attention to someone else's difficulties reflects understanding, commiseration and concern.

Obsession with your weaknesses diverts you from optimal use of time and energy. When you conceal your weaknesses, you stifle your strengths—like Ann, who stifled her wit, her writing talent, her laughter and her love.

In a world filled with lonely people hungry for compassion and acceptance, only those who hide from others and condemn themselves for having bad feelings manage to stay lonely. We could all benefit from giving and accepting more comforting.

A New Direction

Try the following attitude:

I have to accept myself and the responsibility of taking care of my spirit. I'm a sensitive person who's easily hurt by criticism, ridicule and rejection.

But self-respect, not fear, is the guide to a satisfying life. Fear is a warning signal. I need to consider my fears, not blindly run away from them. I must gently but firmly lead the vulnerable child within me to face what frightens me and learn to discriminate between my realistic and unrealistic fears.

If there is a realistic physical danger or risk to my spirit (for example, spending time with someone who insults me or abuses me), then it's my responsibility to avoid that poisonous influence.

But I have to act with courage and directly confront irrational fears that keep me lonely and dissatisfied. I can't let fear bully me into hiding from life.

Being afraid doesn't mean I'm weak. Fear is an opportunity for courage. Facing my fears will make me courageous.

I will find the courage to help the hurt and frightened child within me to face life bravely. It's my only chance for self-respect.

I can use my loneliness to confront my fears. I can extend myself to meet people. I can use my envy to inspire me to do the things I see others doing but have allowed my fears to prevent me from doing. Why not reach out to those who seem to present the least risk of being critical and rejecting?

I can begin by approaching people who also seem insecure. I can say "yes" when friendly people offer their companionship instead of giving in to my fears and hibernating. I can join groups that share the same interests or even the same problems. And I can admit to those who are too assertive and overwhelming that I'm shy and easily hurt, so I need them to be patient and give me time and room to proceed at a slower pace.

It's your job to take care of your vulnerable and wounded spirit, but not to the extreme of hiding from others and life. Begin right now by making a list of groups and individuals you could contact. Make another list of specific things you can do to increase your self-respect. Then, one by one, start contacting the people and doing the things you have listed. It's difficult and frightening to reach out, but the self-respect you'll feel will be worth it and the good results will be a bonus.

PART 8

The Prove Your Worth Traps

CHAPTER 19

The Great American Success Trap

"In the world there are only two tragedies. One is not getting what one wants, and the other is getting it."

Oscar Wilde

Prior To Success:

"If I were successful, I'd no longer doubt myself. I'd feel worthwhile, fulfilled and happy. It makes sense to put success ahead of everything else."

After Success:

"According to everyone else I'm successful. Why don't I feel worthwhile, fulfilled and happy? There must be something wrong with me."

Commonly Associated Features

People in *The Great American Success Trap* may have the following characteristics:

- need to impress others with their accomplishments or appearance
- difficulty accepting comforting
- easily upset by criticism
- tendency to feel dissatisfied even when things are going well
- tendency to be jealous
- addictions to harmful people, substances or habits
- opinionated and defensive
- need to be in control and right, or at least not wrong
- tendency to be disrespectful or inconsiderate, especially to people most important to them.

Addicted to Success

Lawrence, the physics professor and entrepreneur who served as an illustration of *The Biased Against Myself Traps*, also suffers from *The Great American Success Trap*.

Lawrence would vow to cut back on his workaholic pursuit of accomplishment. He promised his wife that the birth of their first child would force him to work less. Lawrence regretted his own loneliness as a child and the poor relationship he had with his father. He didn't want the same to happen with his own son.

Lawerence did arrange a year's sabbatical immediately after his son's birth. But he cut the vacation short and was quickly buried under an avalanche of projects that kept him away from his family.

Later, Lawrence was convinced that each of the following events would compel him to reduce his work schedule: promotion to tenure, his second child, his company becoming a public corporation. But neither the pull of a growing family, nor lifelong academic security, nor the financial freedom of becoming a multimillionaire were enough to enable a leap from the runaway success train taking him farther and farther away from satisfying his spiritual needs for intimacy, rest and play.

Once, after a refreshing family vacation, Lawrence became depressed and unable to concentrate on his work. Lawrence had teased his exhausted spirit with the first vacation he had taken in years. When Lawrence returned to work, his spirit refused to cooperate. He was experiencing a long overdue spiritual rebellion. For forty years, Lawrence had used all his energy desperately trying to fulfill his need to succeed. In the process he had earned fame and fortune. He felt a sense of purpose, but his spirit was starved in every other way.

I urged Lawrence to do some courageous corrective surgery on his life, to put spiritual well-being before achievement. I tried to make him see that a balanced life would provide enough external success to satisfy his need to feel productive and yet allow him to be healthy and rested and to be a loving husband and father.

But Lawrence has been unable to kick his habit. Lawrence's wife, Janice, has become increasingly bitter and irritable. She's retaliated by becoming a success addict herself with less and less time for the children. In Lawrence's presence, I advised his wife to separate from him temporarily to give him a taste of how divorce would feel. I suggested this tactic might shock Lawrence into appreciating what he has been taking for granted and might give Janice more self-respect than her current approach to the problem.

But Janice and Lawrence are caught up in the intoxicating whirl of highly visible success. They are a brilliant, handsome couple, outwardly the most fortunate of people. Janice blames their dissatisfying home life on Lawrence. She intermittently threatens to divorce him or have an affair. She nags and accuses Lawrence. None of this has produced any real improvement.

Meanwhile Lawrence keeps protesting that his family is a higher priority than his work despite overwhelming evidence to the contrary. He openly resents Janice for not being more understanding "for just a little while longer" until he can "get on top of things and spend more time at home."

Escape Route
Exposing the Trap:

The fallacy of *The Great American Success Trap* is that success (in the conventional sense of money, fame, prestige, influence and approval) is the best life has to offer and that you're nothing without it. Success is considered so important that no sacrifice is too great.

The race to success for many people begins in early childhood. Children in many well-to-do families are placed in what are reputed to be the best schools—from preschool to prep school—in order to get them admitted to the best college, so they'll get the best job and marry the "right kind of person." All this maneuvering is considered necessary to achieve the great success required for a satisfying life.

Families of more modest means buy into the myth at great financial sacrifice and sell their children on the magic of external success instead of emphasizing self-respect.

Success can feel wonderful. It certainly beats failure. Success is a necessary ingredient for fulfillment in work. And fulfillment in work is necessary for an overall sense of well-being. You have to have some degree of success to feel meaningful. You need to feel you make a difference, that the world is a better place because you are here.[1]

By definition, success provides money, prestige, fame and influence. Success can also give you a sense of accomplishment and confidence in a particular ability. Financial success allows you freedom—money and time to use as you please. But there are many things success doesn't provide. *Success is not fulfillment.* Success alone is never enough. Many people are successful; far fewer feel fulfilled.

Success alone cannot even provide fulfillment in work. Fulfillment in work is a tall order requiring all of the following ingredients:

- *Self-acceptance:* belief in your inherent worth regardless of success and failures

- *Self-respect:* pride obtained from enthusiastic efforts at some endeavor that seems worth doing

- *Results:* accomplishments that are meaningful to you

- *Success:* rewards provided by others in the form of money, prestige, fame, appreciation or influence

Self-acceptance is the most elusive of these requirements. The greatest success you can imagine won't give you self-acceptance. Self-acceptance is a matter of faith. Doubt about your inherent value is an absolute obstacle to fulfillment. If you doubt your worth, any rewards you receive will feel empty. And accomplishments won't change your sense of yourself. If you become successful you will still doubt yourself, only your success will make you feel like an imposter as well. You will believe that you just happened to do a good thing and got well-compensated for it. (See Chapter 4, *The Self-Doubt Trap: Escape Route,* pp. 42–48.)

---

[1]*For an excellent argument on behalf of the importance of meaning in human psychology see Viktor Frankel's seminal book,* Man's Search for Meaning, *Beacon Press, Boston, 1959.*

Self-doubt is created during childhood by insufficient respect from others and lack of consideration for feelings. The vicious cycle of spiritual neglect begun in childhood is perpetuated in adulthood by Mind Traps like these *Prove Your Worth Traps.* Adults who try to prove their worth through their children's achievements help create self-doubt in their children by neglecting the importance of spiritual well-being.

The pursuit of self-worth through success robs the spirit of its energy and creativity. The single-minded quest can provide a sense of accomplishment and meaning. But a life geared solely towards accomplishment leaves the spirit bankrupt in every other way.

People who accept their intrinsic worth feel no need to prove themselves through appearances, accomplishments or possessions. They are rare people and disarming to those with self-doubt. Often they have modest achievements and routine occupations. They try their best and are proud of their efforts. People who have self-acceptance don't presume to judge others and treat everyone respectfully. But they won't tolerate being treated badly. They generously offer and enthusiastically accept love and comforting.

The next ingredient in the recipe for fulfillment is *self-respect,* a concept that deserves far more attention than it receives. Self-respect is different from self-worth. (See Chapter 4, *The Self-Doubt Trap,* pp. 45−47.)

Self-respect has nothing to do with results and rewards. Self-respect can only be earned by honest, wholehearted efforts at something you feel is worth doing.

Self-respect doesn't depend on success. Self-respect depends exclusively on how hard you've worked at something you believe has merit. The more meritorious the task and the more challenging it is, the more self-respect you earn. Because self-respect comes entirely from efforts, it's completely in your control.

When you work hard all day at a project you believe is

worthwhile, you feel tired but filled with personal satisfaction. You feel a glow of self-respect although you may not have a final product or reward to show for your efforts.

If you have someone else work on your project, you won't earn much self-respect no matter how wonderful the finished product is. And if you were to receive praise for what others did, you would feel undeserving, uncomfortable and unfulfilled.

If you're skeptical about this definition of self-respect and believe it doesn't apply to you, then I encourage you to perform a test: Spend one day doing something that challenges you and that you believe is worth doing—perhaps something you feel would be helpful to someone else. Make certain no one knows that you're the person responsible for the good deed. Then, exhausted from the effort of working hard at something for which you'll receive no material reward, check to see whether you experience any inner satisfaction, self-respect or pride. You be the judge . . .

From self-acceptance and honest efforts we move on to the third ingredient necessary for fulfillment—*results.* Unless what you have accomplished meets your expectations, you won't feel fulfilled.

If other people are delighted with the job you've done and yet you're not satisfied at all, then their approval, no matter how enthusiastic, won't give you a sense of fulfillment. If you record a hit record but personally hate it, spending the money you receive won't be as satisfying as it would have been had *you* been proud of the product. (Although I doubt many of us would turn the money down.)

The final ingredient necessary for fulfillment in work is what is commonly referred to as *success.* Success is indeed sweet. Fulfillment is impossible without validation by others. But all the success in the world feels empty and unfulfilling without the other ingredients: self-acceptance, wholehearted efforts at something you believe is worth doing and results that satisfy you.

Even great success doesn't provide a sense of worth. Did Howard Hughes' billions make him feel secure and worthwhile? Did success reassure Judy Garland? Were wealth, international fame and enthusiastic audiences sufficient for Freddie Prinz, Elvis Presley or Marilyn Monroe?

Those who inherit the advantages of success without having earned it have special problems. To have unearned wealth in a society that worships money is difficult, although few people have sympathy for those who come into the world with silver spoons between their gums. These apparently fortunate people are doomed to dissatisfaction unless they can learn to accept their intrinsic worth and to earn self-respect and rewards through their own efforts at activities that are meaningful to them.

Success earned too easily or by unethical means feels so undeserved it is not only dissatisfying, it can be destructive. A businessman I know accumulated immense wealth by participating in a terrible crime. He is filled with self-disgust, has no close friends and a troubled marriage. He tries to distract himself from self-hatred by making large, charitable contributions and by participating in high-risk business ventures, dangerous sports and extramarital affairs. He asked me the same question he had silently asked himself a thousand times: "Why am I dissatisfied when I have everything a man could ask for?" Perhaps I should have answered him: "For what shall it profit a man, if he shall gain the whole world, and lose his own soul?"[2]

Two terms as president of the United States weren't enough to eliminate Richard Nixon's paranoia about political opponents. *Nixon: The Education of a Politician,*[3] documents the lifelong insecurity and obsessive ambition that

[2] *The Bible, Authorized King James Version, Mark,* 8:36.
[3] Stephen E. Ambrose, *Nixon: The Education of a Politician 1913–1962,* (New York: Simon and Shuster, 1987).

made him willing to use unethical means to get ahead, as noted in a review of the book:

> Mr. Nixon's career seems impelled not by mere desire, but by a powerful necessity, to succeed. The vicious campaign he ran for Congress in 1946 . . . revealed his ruthless single-mindedness. "Of course I knew Jerry Voorhis wasn't a Communist," Mr. Nixon later replied to accusations that he had lied during the campaign. "But . . . I had to win . . . . The important thing is to win." . . . Winning for him seemed to be the test of his character, and even of his identity.[4]

No matter how well you do at impressing others, you will never be able to impress yourself enough to earn self-acceptance. Self-acceptance, like the existence of God, cannot be proven. It requires an act of faith. If you attain success you may find yourself worse off than ever: Success will have failed you. You no longer will have any excuse for your dissatisfaction. Once successful, the success myth is revealed as a false promise—it doesn't provide fulfillment and happiness. Worse, your success will make you feel so flawed and unredeemable that even great accomplishments and the approval of others prove to be insufficient to make you feel good about yourself. Self-doubt reigns supreme. You must either rededicate yourself to the pursuit of further success or turn to unhealthy escapes, like alcohol, drugs, illness or even suicide.

Pursuing success to erase self-doubt and reaping the rewards success provides distract you from the hunger of other needs, like intimacy, rest, recreation, exercise and personal growth.

---

[4]Ronald Steel, "I Had To Win," *The New York Times Book Review,* (April 26, 1987).

The rewards make success addiction an extremely difficult habit to kick. The success myth can keep insecure people going through years and even a lifetime of pain and self-betrayal in the struggle to get to the top and stay there. The pinnacle where one can rest, secure and fulfilled, endlessly recedes into the horizon, like the pot of gold at the end of the rainbow. And the burdens of managing wealth, fame, competition and other complications of success are exhausting. Eventually, success addicts become bankrupt in mind, body and spirit.

It is easy to walk away from failure and try something else. After all, what choice does one have after failure? It's either move on or give up entirely. But few people can voluntarily reduce or give up efforts that are as rewarding as success, especially when their lives are so empty otherwise.

Success addicts are like superb swimmers masterfully battling the current of a powerful river to the cheers of the crowd. They fear they might be pulled back over the falls were they to relax their efforts and join the less ambitious folks who walk along the shore. They see themselves as imposters who would be discovered for who *they fear they are* were they to stop their dazzling performances.

People driven by the need for success, like Lawrence in the example, are confused by their contradictory attitudes. They look down on those who are less successful. Yet they envy other people, too. They regard others as inherently worthy of self-acceptance, whether the other people are successful or not. They judge themselves by a more stringent standard, doubting themselves despite their successes.

Like people addicted to anything else—alcohol, cocaine, food, etc.—for self-doubting success addicts there is no in-between. Withdrawal from the high of success means facing the possibility of a terrifying plunge into despair.

The pathetic image of Howard Hughes protecting himself from any contact, including the risk of encountering microbes on anything he touched and in the air he breathed, could be the classic case of *The Great American Success Trap*. Given that tragic examples of success addicts are common knowledge, why hasn't the success myth been laid to rest? Perhaps it is because materialism in its American version, *The Great American Success Trap*, is the only viable myth we have to live by. Even our religions hew to the bottom line, accumulating immense financial wealth and measuring their success by numbers of followers in the fold.

Only if we accept that each of us has intrinsic worth by virtue of having a unique spirit; only if we honor that spirit by treating it as a sacred gift and a responsibility; only if we act in ways that *feel* right—only then can we feel fulfilled by success. Otherwise, we mistake dissatisfaction as evidence of personal defectiveness, we are possessed by insatiable greed, our successes feel empty and we abuse ourselves and others.

A New Direction:

If you think you may be stuck in *The Great American Success Trap*, then you have already taken the first step in dealing with this powerful addiction. It's unlikely you would admit to it if you weren't dissatisfied. Your discomfort gives you a chance at escaping this trap. Discomfort is an energy bank that you can draw upon to change to a more balanced life with different priorities.

To change you must revise your entire belief system and your daily schedule. Because time is your most valuable commodity, your priorities and how you spend your time are one and the same. (Many people pretend their families are the most important aspect of their lives, yet spend little prime time with them.)

You have been living outside-in, trying to prove you're not flawed by being externally successful. In the process you have largely ignored your spiritual needs. To change you must learn to adopt an inside-out approach to life based on self-acceptance, compassion and self-respect. This new attitude will enable you to discover and use yourself well. For a description of this healthier attitude, please review the following:

To help you reconsider your worth, see Chapter 4, *The Self-Doubt Trap: A New Direction*, pp. 47–48.

To help you revise your attitude toward your discomfort, see Chapter 6, *The "Bad Feelings Are Wrong" Trap: A New Direction*, pp. 68–69.

To help you adopt self-respect as your highest priority, see Chapter 12, *The "People Don't Change" Traps: A New Direction*, pp. 124–126.

To alert you to your needs for intimacy, rest, play and personal growth, see Chapter 24, *Well-Being: The Goal of Personal Change.*

As with any addiction, escape from *The Great American Success Trap* requires help from others—family, therapists, or people who have already overcome their workaholism. Perhaps someday we will have workaholic support groups to help people escape from this socially reinforced but unhealthy addiction.

CHAPTER 20

The Perfectionism Trap

"The Lord seeth not as man seeth; for man looketh on the outward appearance, but the Lord looketh on the heart."

The Bible, Authorized King James Version,
1 Samuel 16: 7

The Perfectionism Trap:

"Maybe I can prove I'm not a bad person by becoming perfect or as close to it as possible."

Commonly Associated Features

People in *The Perfectionism Trap* may have the following characteristics:

- need to impress others with their accomplishments or achievements

- easily upset by criticism

- difficulty accepting honest praise
- tendency to be jealous
- reluctance to expose true feelings
- need to be in control and right, or at least not wrong
- tendency to blame themselves or to blame subordinates or family members

Perfectly Insecure . . .

Vivian is the elegant perfectionistic socialite who served as an example of *The Biased Against Myself Traps.* (See Chapter 11, pp. 109−111.) Behind the glamorous facade of her public life, Vivian led an underground existence. In her secret private life, she tried to appease a hunger for tenderness and understanding she couldn't satisfy in her social whirl.

Vivian's lover, Paul, offered her this other existence. Paul was a small time contractor and artisan. He was quiet, unassuming and devoted to her. Occasionally Paul would take her sons on hunting trips because he felt sorry for them. The boys were sent to prep schools far from home to prepare them for life as wealthy adults. Paul believed they were missing the fun of a normal childhood. Paul would tell Vivian, "Your children will never learn to be sensitive, loving people at those antiseptic finishing schools."

Vivian's affair gave her a taste of what she could have if she were to give up her preoccupation with appearances. It reinforced her envy of women with more normal lives. But she couldn't face the humiliation of being seen as a person who had cheated on her husband. She was afraid of losing her position in the community and becoming just insecure Vivian, known to others as merely another divorcee with money, married to some poor slob. Programmed by her upbringing, Vivian worried more about appearances than spiritual well-being and was dissatisfied with her life as a result.

Perfectionism can have more dire consequences. In June of 1986, newspapers around the country reported the shocking story of twenty-one-year-old Kathy Ormsby. Kathy was attending Carolina State University. She was an A-student, an aspiring medical missionary and a NCAA track-and-field record-holder at 10,000 meters. At her high school's awards banquet, Kathy, the valedictorian with a 99% average, won fourteen awards.

On June 4, two-thirds of the way through an important race, Kathy was in fourth place and within three strides of the lead. Suddenly she bolted away from the course and jumped off a bridge. Kathy severed her spinal cord and is permanently paralyzed from the waist down.

Kathy was a perfectionist in every aspect of her life, from her body (she suffered from an eating disorder) to her grades. She impressed everyone who knew her with her talent, dedication and accomplishments. But apparently she was unable to satisfy herself.

Vivian and Kathy are extreme examples of perfectionism and concern with appearances. More typical examples are overly meticulous housekeepers who make their homes a neat and sanitary living hell, audiophiles who give more attention to sound quality than to music and people who refuse to be seen with hair out of place or with wrinkles in their perfectly coordinated clothing.

Escape Route:
Exposing the Trap:

You are caught in this trap if perfection in any form is one of your highest priorities. People in *The Perfectionism Trap* feel anxious and dissatisfied unless they sense they are closing in on perfection in their physical appearance, their housekeeping, their car or some other external aspect of their lives. They single-mindedly try to impress others in an attempt to relieve their fear of inadequacy. The irony of self-doubt is again evident: If you don't accept your worth as a given, you will be forced to betray your spirit to prove how good you are. But you'll never convince yourself this way. And other people either already accept you or don't give a damn.

Like preoccupation with success, obsessive concern with the appearance of perfection is a self-defeating detour from well-being. It confuses ends with means, appearance with essence. To *pursue* perfection is a noble enterprise. To *require* perfection in order to achieve a sense of worth is pathetic. No matter how good you manage to appear to others, you can't fool yourself. By being perfect you won't be able to erase the fear of personal defectiveness caused by emotional wounds in childhood. In an attempt to impress at any cost, you ignore your own feelings and lose self-respect.

No matter how hard you rub or how powerful the solvent, you can't remove a stain that doesn't exist. There's nothing intrinsically wrong with you and there never has been. A perfectionistic attitude wastes time and energy and reinforces the self-doubt it is attempting to eliminate.

It is impossible to maintain the appearance of perfection for any prolonged period. Even if others are impressed by your appearance and accomplishments, you'll end up wondering, "If I've done so well and impressed everyone else, why do I still feel so insecure?"

Perfectionism also interferes with creativity. If you interpret mistakes as evidence you are flawed, you'll be too cautious to try anything new for fear of making a mess of things. In the obsessive quest for perfection you'll be afraid to take the risks necessary to bring out the best in you.

Mistakes are essential to creativity and growth. To err is not only human, it is essential if you want to discover what you and the world have to offer. Trial and error is nature's way. We can learn by imitating her. Nature doesn't expect every pine cone to produce a tree.

The pursuit of external perfection reflects the human desire for efficiency, predictability and control. We try to control everything. Yet imperfection is often evidence of quality. Small imperfections distinguish natural and hand-made items from mass-produced, machine-made goods. Unpredictability, spontaneity, uniqueness and variety imbue life with vitality.

Perfectionism and satisfaction are mutually contradictory. Perfectionism as an ideal isn't worth the effort except in pursuits requiring the most meticulous workmanship, like spacecraft systems, brain surgery or fine woodwork. Even in these endeavors results are never guaranteed. All anyone can do is to put forth the effort and improve with experience.

Perfection can't prove what is unprovable: your worth. You have worth because you exist with your unique spirit. Like everyone else, you have your strengths and weaknesses. *The only thing that may be wrong with you is the fear that something may be wrong with you.* Perfection, like success, is best considered a goal towards which to aim self-respect generating efforts.

A New Direction:

Perfectionism is an addiction that interferes with well-being. Well-being is an inside-out, not an outside-in process. The approach you need to escape the outside-in focus of this trap is outlined in Chapter 19, *The Great American Success Trap: A New Direction*, pp. 201–202.

If you're serious about escaping *The Perfectionism Trap*, also consider the following attitude:

I'm fed up with allowing what others may think of me to control everything I do. Starting today I'm going to tell the people most important to me what I honestly think and feel. I'll be careful not to blame them or purposely try to upset them. And I'm going to try to get them to be honest with me. Even if things get a little messy, what's true and real is more important than artificial neatness and harmony.

Every day I'm going to yield to an impulse and say or do something silly and out of character. It might be fun to surprise a few people and allow myself to be different. Doing these things will be uncomfortable to begin with. But I'll never change by staying the way I am.

CHAPTER 21

The Conceit Trap

**"Do not make yourself so big,
you are not so small."**

Jewish Proverb

The Conceit Trap:

"As long as I keep reminding everyone that I've got more going for me than most people, I don't have to worry about not being good enough."

Commonly Associated Features

People in the *Conceit Trap* may have some of the following characteristics:

- need to impress others with their accomplishments or appearance
- tendency to be jealous
- easily upset by criticism, though they try to hide it
- tendency to be opinionated and defensive
- need to be in control and right, or at least not wrong

So Vain

Fred, a successful insurance agent, was always blowing his own horn. His wife Ellen, couldn't stand his incessant lying and boasting any longer. She described her frustration to me:

Fred pretends we have tons of money. I ask him if it's okay to buy something and he tells me to go ahead and buy it. Then the bank calls because we don't have enough to cover the check. So I tell him and he says he'll take care of it right away. Two days later there's still no money in the account. It's humiliating. If he'd just explain we're short of cash I wouldn't mind at all. It's the lying that drives me crazy!

He'll boast about wonderful job offers he has turned down. But what he's referring to are nothing more than casual conversations he's initiated with people he envies. They never pick up on the feelers he puts out and I know it hurts his pride. Why does he pretend *they* have approached *him*? He really is talented and successful. Why does he feel he has to exaggerate his accomplishments?

And he's so damn critical of everyone except himself. He calls anyone who is obviously more successful than he is a jerk and anyone less successful a loser. But if *he* fails or is criticized he gets terribly depressed and feels sorry for himself.

Fred drives custom-made cars, wears the most expensive clothes and feels he has to be better than everyone else. He's the most self-centered person I've ever met. I married him because he seemed warm, tender, sensitive and brilliant. And he is. I just hate his b.s.!

When Fred and I talked alone later, he seemed relieved to confess his lifelong insecurities. He described his childhood briefly: Although an excellent student and above-average athlete, he was lonely. He kept trying to impress others in hope of being accepted, but it didn't work. He pretended not to care and to look down on his classmates, but being an outsider hurt.

The pattern had continued into adulthood with some added twists: Fred developed a compulsive need to seduce women and to gamble. He still had no close friends. And now he had disappointed Ellen so much she wouldn't live with him unless he consulted a psychiatrist.

We all come by who we are for good reasons. Fred's early family life was emotionally cold. His parents were hard-working people who recognized their son's intelligence and pushed him to achieve. He felt they were relentlessly critical and impossible to satisfy.

Escape Route
Exposing the Trap:

Conceit, like shyness, is a futile attempt to compensate for self-doubt. Conceit offends people and makes you lonely.

One way people manifest their conceit and insecurity is by constantly denigrating the attributes and accomplishments of others. In an attempt to build themselves up, they put everyone and everything else down.

Another variety of conceit could be called *The "I Already Know Anything That's Important" Trap.* When people in this trap are told of something new, they either claim to already know about the new information or dismiss it as nonsense. Often associated with *The "Feelings Are Foolish" Trap,* this brand of conceit reflects fear of being out of control, wrong and hurt. If you ignore anything that doesn't fit your preexisting way of thinking, you'll remain stuck exactly where you are and always have been. You may become more successful doing what you already know, but you won't grow.

If you boast about your talents and accomplishments, look down on others or claim to know everything that's important, then, despite your gifts and successes, you doubt your own worth.

Achievements come from a combination of inborn talent, for which you deserve no credit whatsoever, and your efforts, for which you deserve full credit.

TALENTS + EFFORTS ⟶ RESULTS + REWARDS

Pride in wholehearted efforts and fulfillment from success are nourishing to the spirit. But waving your accomplishments and abilities in front of others irritates them and keeps you lonely.

There is confusion about humility in our culture. Polite society admires those who are modest. But modesty by successful people can be a facade meant to please others and hide self-doubt. (See *The "You Flatter Me" Trap,* Chapter 11.) False modesty by talented people who have achieved a great deal can be just as condescending to those of lesser talent and accomplishment as conceit. By denigrating their own abilities and accomplishments, high achievers indirectly insult those who have achieved less but have done the best they could.

A more honest and healthier approach than conceit or false modesty is to *take justifiable pride in dedicated efforts and humbly rejoice in inherited talents.*

A New Direction:

Learn to put self-acceptance and self-respect ahead of results and rewards. Stop worrying about what others may think and concentrate on how you feel about yourself. No amount of approval from anyone else will feel as satisfying as self-acceptance supplemented by regular doses of self-respect.

For the next few weeks, experiment with not talking about yourself, not trying to prove how much you know and not putting other people down. Encourage others to talk about what *they* are interested in and listen carefully enough to be able to summarize out loud what they've said. If they ask about you, be brief and understated. Then bring the conversation back to the other person as quickly as you can. Begin to look for honest positive things you can say about others. Experiment with openmindedness when introduced to new ideas and opinions that differ from your own.

For additional recommendations, see Chapter 19, *The Great American Success Trap: A New Direction,* pp. 201–202.

CHAPTER 22

The "I'm Right and You're Wrong" Trap

> "How strange it is to see with how much passion
> People see things only in their own fashion!"
>
> Molière

The "I'm Right and You're Wrong" Trap:

"Only one of us can be right—either I'm right and you're wrong or (God forbid) you're right and I'm wrong. Being wrong about something makes me feel something is wrong with me."

Commonly Associated Features

People in *The "I'm Right and You're Wrong" Trap* may have the following characteristics:

- tendency to be opinionated and defensive
- need to be in control and right, or at least not wrong
- tendency to be disrespectful and inconsiderate, especially to people most important to them
- critical and blaming of others
- need to impress others with their accomplishments or appearance
- easily upset by criticism
- seldom tender or warm

Examples

Few couples are entirely free of *The "I'm Right and You're Wrong" Trap.* For specific examples of this trap in action see the Chapter 14, *The Blame Trap: Climbing Out of the Rut,* pp. 140–143, and Chapter 12, *The "People Don't Change" Traps: Playing House,* pp. 118–121.

Escape Route
Exposing the Trap

This *Prove Your Worth Trap* is a form of conceit used in relationships by insecure people. Relationships won't work if you use them to reassure yourself about your worth—in this case by proving the other person is wrong about something, or worse, everything.

If you emerge from childhood still concerned about self-worth, then defeating someone else can temporarily reassure you that you're not a loser. This, of course, is destructive foolishness. Although disagreements are inevitable, the need to be right and win is incompatible with the spirit of partnership.

Unlike scientific truth, there are as many valid personal truths as there are human beings on this earth. Scientific truths are devoid of feelings. Personal truths are inseparable from feelings.

The bonds that unite people are respect and consideration about each other's feelings, not rational agreements. (To pretend agreement merely to appease one another destroys any chance of intimacy.) Defeating a partner undermines a relationship. Your partner becomes a loser who resents you for winning, so you become a loser too.

Whether they realize it or not, couples who are painfully ensnarled in *The "I'm Right and You're Wrong" Trap* have agendas other than intimacy. A hidden purpose of the struggle to be right is to *avoid the risk* of intimacy. For people with a history of being badly hurt and inadequately comforted, rejection and loss are too painful to endure. Regular heated arguments provide passionate interaction without risking trust and closeness (a partnership style memorialized in Edward Albee's *Who's Afraid of Virginia Woolf?*). In these fights, everyone ultimately loses. Each battle creates wounds and lasting scars.

To struggle for self-respect and compassionate treatment is healthy; to try to defeat each other isn't. This trap's practitioners miss the point of relationships: to support and encourage each other, to share good times, buffer the bad and enrich each others' lives—*even if it will hurt like hell when the relationship ends.* One way or another all relationships must end eventually. So even if comforting feels awkward, it's important to learn how to accept comforting and to have supportive people available in your life.

Occasional disagreements can be energizing. Thorough and considerate discussion of different views can enrich your relationship. This requires an honest attempt to understand what it feels like to be the other person, a fascinating challenge if you approach your differences with curiosity about each other's position.

Creative resolution of disagreements requires careful packaging of your words so you are *explaining yourself* instead of *refuting your partner.* The more honest and the gentler you are at expressing what you think and feel without insisting you're right, the more intimacy you'll find and the less lonely you'll be.

A New Direction

Accept that there is no right or wrong in relationships:

I'm far better off trying to become an expert on my partner's thoughts and feelings than trying to prove I'm right. If we show we understand and care about each other's thoughts and feelings, we'll feel closer and more trusting. Exploring each other's position doesn't imply agreement, but it will ensure intimacy.

Anger is always based on hurt, fear and the feeling that one is not respected. Anger is best treated as a cry for help instead of an attack. If we can learn to comfort the pain behind the anger, even if the anger is directed at one another, we'll remain close and become even closer. No defensiveness is necessary. We're not here to judge each other's worth. Our own worth is up to each of us to accept on faith. This attitude is worth the effort it requires.

Instead of attacking each other, we can use disagreements as opportunities to ferret out hidden needs and resentments that keep us apart. We need to nurture the child within each of us. The issue must shift from "Who's right?" to "What can we do to help one another?"

We can begin today by changing how we talk to each

other. Maybe we can admit how easily hurt we both are and how much we'd appreciate considerate treatment.

A caveat—this approach works so well that intimacy often grows too rapidly for couples lacking experience with trust and closeness. If you have more experience with pain and loneliness than with comforting, openness can feel like too great a risk. For suggestions on how to handle the fear of intimacy, see Chapter 16, *The Rejection Trap: A New Direction,* pp. 170–171.

CHAPTER 23

The "Your Happiness Is My Responsibility" Trap

"The burning conviction that we have a holy duty toward others is often a way of attaching our drowning selves to a passing raft."

Eric Hoffer

The "Your Happiness Is My Responsibility Trap":

"I feel like I should take care of anyone who is unhappy. I have trouble saying no, regardless of what I really think, feel and want."

Commonly Associated Features

People in *The "Your Happiness is My Responsibility" Trap* may have the following characteristics:

- likely to place others' needs and wishes ahead of their own

- difficulty making decisions and dependent on the opinions of others

- easily upset by criticism

- tendency to avoid confrontations at almost any cost

- reluctance to expose true feelings

Make Someone Happy

Three people will illustrate The "Your Happiness Is My Responsibility" Trap: Marilyn Monroe, my father and one of my clients. All had severe self-doubt and tried to earn a sense of worth by pleasing others.

Marilyn Monroe's childhood was fertile ground for cultivation of self-doubt. Marilyn suffered repeated rejections and endured her pain alone. She was an illegitimate child. Her father abandoned her and when she eventually located him, he refused to see her. Marilyn's mother was placed in a psychiatric hospital and ultimately died in an institution. Marilyn lived in over half a dozen foster homes and one orphanage. And most biographers find no reason to doubt her allegations that she was sexually molested as a child on at least two occasions.[1]

Like most people who lacked consistent comforting in childhood, Marilyn mistook pain as evidence of personal defectiveness instead of interpreting it as a message from her wounded spirit. Early in her career, she turned to alcohol and drugs to numb her fear and hurt.

Marilyn relied on her beauty, warmth and seductive vulnerability to obtain approval. She had sex with many highly successful men. In retrospect, she admitted she derived no

[1]Gloria Steinem, *Marilyn*, (New York: Henry Holt and Co., 1986).

sensuous pleasure from these encounters. Marilyn became involved with these men because of their prestige and because she hoped they would take care of her. Ultimately each of them rejected her.

Marilyn's husbands were strong and domineering men who became critical and rejecting. Although her agent was always considerate and loving, and though they had an affair, Marilyn never felt romantic love for him and refused his marriage proposals.

As an adult, Marilyn continued to experience the pain and rejection she had grown up with. She felt like a failure, despite her appeal and fame. Marilyn never stopped trying to please people and escape her despair. She finally succeeded, not in earning self-acceptance, but in taking her own life.

Toni, my client, represents a more commonplace example of *The "Your Happiness Is My Responsibility" Trap:* Toni sacrificed herself for her husband and his children in an attempt to feel worthwhile.

Toni married a widower with two young daughters. Her husband, Vic, was a construction foreman, a church deacon and a devoted father. At first, the marriage went well. Toni was a loving mother to his children and she sensed Vic's unexpressed appreciation.

But after Toni and Vic discovered they couldn't have a child of their own and his low sperm count was identified as the probable cause, Vic no longer wanted to have sex. This deprived Toni of the only overt affection Vic had ever offered her. From that point on they had a polite but perfunctory relationship. Vic and Toni never discussed anything but superficialities for the next eight years.

During those eight years, Toni devoted herself to being a good mother and became heavily involved in church activities. Toni frequently donated her time and was widely respected in the community. But she felt worn out and began putting on weight. Toni finally shocked herself into seeking help when she began having an affair with a friend's husband.

As the final example, I turn to my late father. My father left Lithuania in his early twenties with little formal education and work experience only as a farm hand. He came to Canada, worked as an assistant butcher in his cousin's shop, and later became a bakery owner.

There was nothing my father wouldn't do for people. I once commented how good the shirt he was wearing looked on him. To my dismay he then literally tried to give me the shirt right off his back. My father's need to please was so extreme that he was unwilling to say or do anything when he discovered his younger brother had stolen thousands of dollars of merchandise from him.

My dad was intelligent, sensitive and kind. He was successful in business despite his lack of education. But he never overcame his self-doubt, his loneliness and his unrelenting, self-sacrificing efforts to please.

My father taught me how to be a demonstratively loving man. That was his greatest gift to me. But he was a poor model of compassion and responsibility for oneself. Because he always put others first, he rarely satisfied himself. He would silently and endlessly wait for the payoffs he hoped his generosity would provide instead of taking responsibility to make certain his spirit received what it needed. And, inadvertently, his indulgence of my every whim during childhood encouraged me later to expect others (especially my wife) to make me happy.

Escape Route
Exposing the Trap

The "Your Happiness Is My Responsibility" Trap is an attempt to prove one's worth in the arena of personal relationships. People in this trap pursue success in the form of arranging for other people's happiness. This effort to please is not based on compassionate altruistic motives. *The "Your Happiness Is My Responsibility" Trap* is a way to compensate for feelings of inadequacy and to avoid criticism and rejection.

If you always feel the need to please others, you did not receive enough tenderness, understanding and comforting to satisfy your spirit during childhood. You were hurt and lonely often enough to have developed significant self-doubt. As a result, you look for warmth and approval to reassure you. And you assiduously avoid unhappiness because it reminds you of unpleasant childhood scenes that made you feel defective.

One of my clients vividly remembers his parents' repeated threats to send him to an orphange each time they were upset with him. He is disarmingly charming and ingratiating, but sadly lacking in self-respect.

Like the quest for perfection and success, attempts to vindicate yourself by pleasing others are doomed. You can't make anyone else's happiness your responsibility for long without betraying yourself. Other people's happiness and your self-respect can't both be your *highest* priorities. Self-respect must come first. In your obsession with pleasing others, you abdicate responsibility for your own spiritual well-being and you encourage others to rely on you instead of taking responsibility for themselves.

If you try to please and ask for nothing in return, people eventually take you for granted. They lose respect for you because you look pathetic bending over backward to appease them. Even if you do receive their appreciation, it won't be enough to reassure yourself and you probably won't be able to accept it. Eventually you'll resent each other because you can't always please despite your best efforts.

Sharing life's pain and pleasure is what intimacy is all

about. But manipulative pleasers are too uncomfortable with other people's pain to be good at comforting. And their dissatisfaction with themselves makes it difficult for them to wholeheartedly rejoice when others are feeling good. People in this trap need others to feel bad so they can help out and so they can be distracted from their own dissatisfaction.

You won't find intimacy by pleasing people or trying to solve their problems. Trying to solve people's problems is a skilled occupation practiced by people who get paid for what they do. If you try to please others to get appreciation without clearly being asked to do so, all you get is resentment for interfering and presuming you can solve everything. Most people (including children) would rather be comforted and understood than protected and controlled.

Putting your spiritual well-being first isn't selfishness. It's fairness. Although you can't feel self-respect if you ignore the feelings of those you care about, *your* inner child needs equal time. You deserve consideration too.

A New Direction

Nothing feels better than being considerate to others and cared about in return. There's no more selfish *and* benevolent way to live. The better you get at understanding what others feel and showing you care, the more you can expect and, if necessary, even demand in return. Learn to *care about* others' feelings rather than trying to *take care of* them.

Adopt the following attitude:

My primary responsibility is to take care of my own spirit. That means earning self-respect and taking care of my needs as best I can by listening to what my feelings are telling me.

Sometimes a good relationship may require me to get tough and use leverage. I may need to use sanctions, like depriving another person of something I provide for a while to prove I mean business. Eventually, if tactical weapons fail, I may be forced to resort to strategic interventions, perhaps even ending the relationship completely.

Spiritual well-being, like charity, begins at home.

PART 9

The Self-Change Program

Introduction to the Self-Change Program

"**The important thing is this: to be able at any moment to sacrifice what we are for what we could become.**"

Charles Du Bos

The final three chapters of *Mind Traps* are designed to help you assess what you want to change about your life and take the steps necessary to accomplish your goals.

Chapter 24, *Well-Being: The Goal of Personal Change*, proposes an ideal of well-being. It describes five ingredients necessary for a sense of well-being and may help you clarify what could be missing in your life.

Chapter 25, *Changing Attitudes,* offers a way of looking at yourself which will help you grow from who you are to who you'd prefer to be.

Chapter 26, *Self-Change: Step-by-Step,* explains how to use this book as a guide in a step-by-step program for personal change.

CHAPTER 24

Well-Being: The Goal of Personal Change

"Believe that life is worth living and your belief will help you create the fact."

William James

How good can life be? One version of the good life is that depicted in the media and epitomized in television's *Lifestyles of the Rich and Famous*. Despite repeated exposés of the tragic and painful lives of celebrities who apparently had it all—wealth, power, fame—the myth persists: Get to the top any way you can without getting caught if you want the best life has to offer.

There are, of course, other definitions of the good life that emphasize philosophical, psychological and religious values rather than material rewards. I have chosen to present some practical definitions and formulas designed to help anyone who wants to achieve a better life, based on experience from my personal life and practice.

If the following attitudes and ways of acting make sense

to you, you can experiment with them. The crucial test is your own experience. If you want a better life, you must be curious and take risks; you must find the courage to try out different attitudes and actions.

A Recipe for Well-Being

What is well-being? How does it feel? How can you arrange for it?

Well-being has at least five essential requirements:

- Fulfillment in your endeavors

- Intimacy in relationships

- Personal growth

- Rest

- Recreation

These five elements are necessary for a sense of well-being—to feel satisfied and grateful to be alive and able to enjoy another day.

Well-being doesn't imply invulnerability to emotional pain or physical invincibility. And well-being doesn't mean the absence of fear. To be free of fear requires intoxication or unconsciousness.

Well-being also isn't the same as happiness. Happiness can be a passive experience. Events like winning a lottery can make you happier temporarily even if you don't feel good about yourself. *Well-being requires deliberately choosing ways of acting guided by one's feelings and values.*

Well-being requires one to *deliberately* lead one's life in compassionate, self-respecting ways. Occasional happy moments can happen to anyone. Well-being can only come to people who arrange for it. Even if you prepare carefully for well-being you can rarely satisfy all five requirements simultaneously.

You may be able to supplement the list of five requirements for well-being with additional needs you personally must satisfy to feel good. (For example, there are those who have learned to require ready access to a telephone, a shopping center, or even a certain brand of bottled water.) But whatever your particular needs, all five of the ingredients listed are essential for everyone.

Fulfillment in Your Endeavors

All of the following ingredients are necessary for fulfillment in work:

- *Self-Acceptance:* unconditional belief in one's inherent worth regardless of one's successes and failures

- *Self-Respect:* pride obtained from honest enthusiastic efforts at some endeavor that seems worth doing

- *Results:* personally meaningful accomplishments

- *Rewards:* affirmations provided by others in the form of money, prestige, fame, appreciation or influence

Intimacy

Intimacy, the second of the five components necessary for well-being, refers to mutual understanding and caring in a relationship. Intimacy is widely discussed and desired but rarely achieved. Intimacy is a tall order with its own prerequisites:

- *Self-Acceptance*
- *Respect*
- *Understanding*
- *Caring*

attitudes towards oneself and others

Like fulfillment in work, intimacy requires you to accept your inherent worth unconditionally. To have any hope of intimacy you must believe you are a good and decent person at heart, if not always in your actions.

If you can't look into your own eyes with a deep sense of caring, how can you feel comfortable when someone you love gazes lovingly into your eyes? (See *The Mirror Exercise*, p. 256). How can you risk revealing yourself to someone else and feel worthy of that person's love if you're afraid you may be defective? And how can you believe your love is worth anything if you doubt whether you're worth much?

Intimacy is rare. Few people feel well-understood and deeply cared about. Loneliness is common. At some level each of us feels different from everyone else. And we are. Each of us experiences the world—even the same movie— in a different way. Some isolation and loneliness is inevitable. But many people are far more isolated and lonely than necessary because of self-doubt.

Intimacy depends on how you relate to yourself and others. You can't have intimacy with someone else if you don't have intimacy with yourself. And you can't have intimacy if you don't reach out and expose yourself to others. Compassion and self-respect are necessary for achieving self-acceptance and intimacy.

If you are willing to work on achieving intimacy and eliminating self-doubt, the cooperation of a partner who wants the same can accelerate the process. Understanding, caring and encouragement provide the support a couple needs to grow as individuals and to build a future together.

Personal Growth

Personal growth is the expansion of one's experience and abilities. Growth comes from experimenting with new attitudes and actions likely to satisfy your needs and increase your self-respect.

An excellent way to grow is to risk placing yourself in situations you have never experienced or not yet mastered. Challenging yourself pushes you to rise to the occasion and learn new ways of living. If you stretch yourself to master unfamiliar situations—such as learning to stand up for yourself or being more open about your feelings—you will keep changing into someone new, someone who feels like a different person, more self-respecting, compassionate and capable than before. It is immensely satisfying to feel increasingly competent and perhaps slightly embarrassed by the person you used to be.

Rest

Humans need time to recharge. Obviously we require sleep, but we also need to spend time being *awake and resting.* This awake but resting stage might be compared to the warming up of a car engine.

Rest or relaxation is a distinct state of mind. You are awake but mentally passive. You note but don't analyze, categorize or judge. You are peacefully affected by your perceptions but you make no attempt to control or influence anything. Your mind merely notes and floats, floats and notes, without bothering to pursue your thoughts.

People who work the hardest and need the most rest often have the greatest difficulty arranging for time off. Most ambitious people find it impossible to just sit and stare at a fire, the ocean or a painting and relax. Many depressed people have not had a vacation in a year or more.

The popularity of meditation courses over the past twenty-five years may be related to the need for restorative time that is free from everyday demands. Meditation and some other forms of rest take practice. Practice is required to learn to make the jump from goal-oriented thinking to restful consciousness. Because escapes like alcohol, drugs and television require less effort than meditating or contemplation of nature, they are more widely practiced. But they are not high quality rest.

Recreation

"Man is wholly himself only when he plays."

F. Schiller

Webster's Third New International Dictionary defines recreation as "refreshment of the strength and spirits after toil: diversion, play." Play is a restorative activity that has no product or result other than the benefits derived from participating in the activity itself. For play to refresh, it must be performed solely for the sake of playing.

Rest regenerates, play rejuvenates. Play can release your inner child and encourage intuition and creativity. Unfortunately, recreation is even more honored in the breach and less in the observance than rest.

If you take time out from your struggle with a difficult problem to exercise, rest, sleep or play, a solution often will become apparent. For example, Poincaré, a great French mathematician, was frustrated by his inability to come up with some equations, and decided to take a vacation. On the first day of his vacation, as he boarded a bus, several equations suddenly occurred to him. He immediately wrote them down and put them away. When he returned home after the vacation he found that they were exactly what he had been trying to come up with for months prior to his holiday.

Not everything we call "play" is play. Golf, racquetball, tennis—competitive sports and all activities in which you measure time, points, distance or anything else—may be good for your body and divert you from everyday concerns, but they are *not* play!

Jogging to get into condition, competition to determine who is better, keeping score (even if only to determine whether one is improving with practice)—all these accomplish something other than restoring your spirit. Even if by measuring you are just trying to make things interesting, keeping score adulterates play and reduces its spiritual benefits.

When, like a happy child playing in a sandbox, you lose yourself in some activity like dancing or strolling on the beach, you enrich your spirit. Like rest, true play involves a different state of mind than that involved in managing everyday life. To play golf without keeping score just to enjoy the walk, the surrounding and the comradery; to hike in the woods but not record the number of birds you can identify or how far you've gone; to simply relish the experience of doing what you're doing—these are rare experiences for most hard working adults.

I once offered this definition of recreation in a workshop to a group of physicians. "Would just collecting seashells qualify as play?" a member of the audience asked. Before I could answer, the man sitting beside the ostensibly playful beachcomber blurted out, "What if the guy keeps boasting about having one of the world's finest private collections?"

Is Well-Being Possible?

Can everyone change enough to achieve well-being? Intimacy in relationships, fulfillment in work, growth, rest and relaxation . . . there seem to be so many prerequisites. Is well-being really possible?

Definitely—but not every moment, not even every day, week or month. Happiness and well-being come and go even in the best of lives. Only rarely are the five conditions for well-being simultaneously present in anyone's life.

Well-being depends upon being in a state of readiness to grab it for brief periods of time as opportunities arise. Crucial to this state of readiness is self-acceptance, that is, the elimination of self-doubt about one's worth and of the self-defeating attitudes, the Mind Traps, that self-doubt creates.

So this book has come full circle, ending on the issue with which it began, self-doubt and its splendid alternative, self-acceptance. Without self-acceptance, well-being is impossible. But even with self-acceptance, well-being is a challenge. No matter how much success you may have, how deeply you are loved or how physically fit you are, with self-doubt you just won't feel you deserve well-being.

The more severe your childhood wounds are, the greater your self-doubt and the more difficult and frightening it will be for you to accept your worth. However, you *can* achieve self-acceptance. You just have to want it badly enough to confront your fears and try enthusiastically to be the person you want to be, making use of any help you can get along the way.

Once you have taken the steps necessary and found self-acceptance, you'll never lose it again. That's guaranteed. You'll be amazed you ever questioned your worth in the first place. You'll continue to gain or lose self-respect from moment-to-moment, in response to your moment-to-moment choice of actions, but your belief in your own worth will remain. Self-acceptance will become a permanent part of your identity, just as self-doubt used to be. Once you understand that your worth was given to you, it no longer makes any sense to question it, no matter what you do or what happens to you.

With self-acceptance you no longer see your discomfort as evidence of your defectiveness. Once self-doubt disappears, discomfort is seen for what it is, evidence that your spirit is hurting and asking for you to do something to help. Your feelings become an invaluable internal guidance system.

Going from self-doubt to self-acceptance is like accurately recalibrating the compass that was misguiding your life. If you don't have self-acceptance, it is difficult to act or be treated too well for too long. Once you achieve self-acceptance, it will be difficult to act or be treated badly for very long. *The Familiarity Principle* now begins to work on your behalf instead of against you. You can no longer stand to act or be treated with disrespect without becoming uncomfortable and taking remedial action.

Self-acceptance is the solid foundation necessary for a good life and therefore must be the primary goal of self-change. The final two chapters explain how you can use this book as a tool to achieve self-acceptance and a chance at some well-being.

CHAPTER 25

Changing Attitudes

"Nothing is permanent but change."

Heraclitus

Example

To illustrate the ideas in this chapter, I will refer to Alex's experiences at self-change. Alex was the person used as an example of *The "Bad Feelings Are Wrong" Trap* (Chapter 6).

Like most people who consult therapists, Alex did not come in with the primary goal of changing himself. He was in almost continuous pain from his headaches and wanted relief anyway he could get it. Alex had to be convinced that to enjoy a more satisfying life he would have to change significantly.

"All changes, even the most longed for, have their melancholy; for what we leave behind us is a part of ourselves; we must die to one life before we can enter into another!"

Anatole France

Active Change

All things change, but people can *choose* to change themselves. Active change—self-change—is different from passive change. In passive change your actions may change even though you aren't aware of the changes. In active change, you must deliberately act as if you are the person you would prefer to be.

There is nothing unusual about self-change, we all have done it—learned to ride a bicycle, speak a foreign language, or acquired the skills of a profession. We have all experienced the difficulties involved in learning something new. These difficulties in part have to do with the complexity of the skills we wish to acquire. But some of the struggle involved in learning is due to the resistance we feel to letting go of who we are and allowing ourselves to become someone different and better than we believe we could be. To overcome this resistance, we must learn to stand back and compassionately reconsider our beliefs about ourselves.

To give up being who you are and become someone you have never known is one of life's most difficult challenges. The old you does not leave willingly. It wants desperately to survive no matter how unhappy it is, and it will put up a hell of a fight. The habitual self (see Chapter 3, *The Familiarity Principle*) can be so insistent that some people tortured by self-hatred and emotional pain commit suicide because they cannot imagine changing and feeling better.

For example, Alex was afraid he would die from whatever was causing his headaches. Yet he kept thinking about suicide. He wanted to escape not only his physical pain, but his fear and despair about being defective. Alex was haunted by an increasing sense of futility. He was losing hope that anything could make him feel better.

The more central to your sense of identity the aspect of yourself you wish to change is the more terrifying the change and the more you will resist it. For example, where you live is more amenable to change than your gender orientation (unless you happen to be an inveterate

Manhattanite, who might prefer a sex change to a move off the island).

Your sense of worth, self-doubt, is part of your core sense of who you are and is difficult to change. But unless you do what is necessary to change your sense of worth from self-doubt to self-acceptance, any other changes you may make will leave you dissatisfied with yourself and your life.

The shift to self-acceptance depends on your *attitude* and *efforts, not your achievements.* The rest of this chapter describes the attitudes and efforts necessary to change from self-doubt to self-acceptance.

Compassionate Self-Observation

Self-initiated, self-directed change is a paradox. If you wish to become a different person, *you* must change *you.* The paradox of self-change comes from having to be both the agent and object of your changes. If you are successful at changing yourself, then the you who initiated the change will no longer exist.

The solution to the paradox of self-change resides in the human capacity to self-observe. Our minds have the ability to divide our attention. We can stand back and observe ourselves while we are doing something else. This ability to see ourselves allows us to conceive of becoming someone new and different.

Your capacity to have an observing self who can observe the acting self is what makes it possible for you to change. Your observing self enables you to consider various new identities and find one enticing enough to motivate you to abandon your familiar identity.

Self-Awareness versus Self-Consciousness

If you want to get rid of your familiar identity, you must struggle to avoid self-consciousness. Unless you work deliberately to avoid it, self-consciousness will make you uncomfortable when you begin to act differently than you're accustomed to. Your self-conscious self will ask you, "Who are you trying to kid acting as if you're different than you've always been?" Self-consciousness keeps your self-observer in the full-time employ of the Familiarity Principle, loyally working to maintain your habitual identity.

Fortunately, your self-observer is capable of better things. At the very least you can rise above your habitual bias of self-doubt. You can shift from being your own opponent to being an objective and fair referee. But you can rise even above that. Eventually you can move from neutrality about yourself to being on your own side. With practice, your capacity for self-awareness can allow you to go from objectivity to having compassion and enthusiasm for yourself.

You cooperate most with people who care what you think and who are interested in helping you develop your talents. It follows that you will give yourself the best chance at self-change if you learn to appreciate your own talents, sensitivities and vulnerabilities.

Alex managed to shift in self-observation from being negative and self-conscious to compassionate and encouraging. This was the key to his recovery.

If you want a model for the self-observer within you whose job it is to help you change and grow, you can emulate spiritual leaders who have always urged people to emphasize the best in themselves and others. If these models are too intimidating, try imagining a kindly grandparent or a tough coach with a gentle heart—someone who has seen and heard it all, who is fooled by nothing, but can understand and forgive anything, who has more faith in your potential than you ever have had and who expects you to give yourself a better chance in the future.

By developing your self-observer into a compassionate observer, you will solve the two major obstacles to self-change: the self-changing-self paradox and the fear of losing your familiar identity. Your compassionate observer is a self you can turn to and rely on while you change for the better. It can be the dependable guiding part of you. The you who changes in self-change is not the only you, so you won't have to lose all of yourself when you change. The compassionate self-observer will be there to observe everything in and around you and to urge you to take better care of your spirit.

Your compassionate observer and your spirit are relatively unchanging. However, your compassionate observer will become more competent as you use it, and your spirit will reveal more of itself as you courageously experiment with self-change.

Your self-observer can use imagination to help you change. The more you can imagine the possibility of a new you who you would prefer to be, the more likely you are to change. Athletes and musicians have demonstrated the effectiveness of creating a mental picture of the performance they aspire to. Rehearsing optimal performances in their minds can improve their actual performances. By imagining and practicing, you will progress towards your ideal.

Compassion for self conflicts with self-doubt. If you doubt your worth, you'll find it hard to believe you deserve to be cheered on to a better life. Adopting a consistent compassionate observer attitude towards yourself is the single most difficult and crucial ingredient of the self-change process.

(*See the compassionate observer diagram on page 248.*)

Self-Respect Generating Actions

The two important guidelines for your new actions are satisfaction of your needs and self-respect. To persist at self-change you must be more concerned about what your spirit needs than what others think. You must be willing to take loving responsibility for your own needs. At the same time, you need to feel right about the ways you're trying to change.

THE COMPASSIONATE OBSERVER

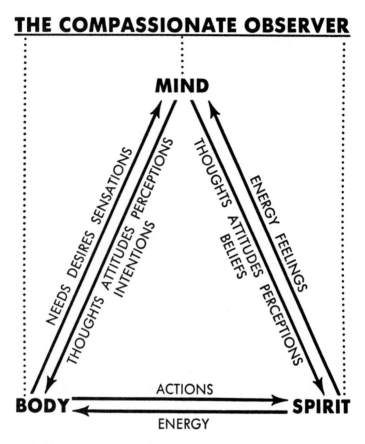

MIND

NEEDS DESIRES SENSATIONS

THOUGHTS ATTITUDES PERCEPTIONS INTENTIONS

THOUGHTS ATTITUDES BELIEFS

ENERGY FEELINGS

THOUGHTS ATTITUDES PERCEPTIONS

ACTIONS

BODY ⟶ **SPIRIT**

ENERGY

Self-respect comes from enthusiastic efforts, not from results. It comes from trying to accomplish what you believe is worthwhile, from doing what makes you feel better about yourself merely because you tried. Whether or not your efforts are successful, the more difficult and frightening the challenge and the harder you try, the more self-respect you'll earn.

Challenging yourself is also important because your spirit needs to have its talents used. Innate ability cries out to be exercised and refined. Unless you use your inborn capacities you'll feel the discomfort that comes from not stretching to the limits of your capabilities and from wasting your talents. To rid yourself of this discomfort and take care of your spirit you must try self-respect generating experiments. Responding to your spirit's need to have its talents used will result in continual change and growth.

By monitoring his feelings while experimenting with different occupations, Alex found that being a landscape architect was more challenging and in harmony with his spirit than being a draftsman.

"The interval between the decay of the old and the formation and establishment of the new constitutes a period of transition, which must always be one of uncertainty, confusion, error, and wild and fierce fanaticism."

John C. Calhoun

"A child-like man is not a man whose development has been arrested; on the contrary he is a man who has given himself a chance of continuing to develop long after most adults have muffled themselves in the cocoon of middle-aged habit and convention."

Aldous Huxley

The Need for Passion

Unable to type, you sit at the keyboard pretending to be a typist; unable to ski, you make stilted efforts at copying the motions of accomplished skiers, unble to speak a foreign language, you mouth the words in imitation of a native speaker.

You must keep practicing being your new, more self-respecting self until it is no longer an act. This deliberate and awkward phase is difficult but essential for any significant self-change. You can't change without changing how you act. You have changed yourself when you have changed *how you are and who you believe you are.* Change in self-concept will only come after you have had a great deal of practice acting like a different person.

The more passionately you throw yourself into the affectation of being who you'd like to be, the better you are at imagining yourself as the new person, the more successful you are at suspending your disbelief about being whoever you would like to become, and the less self-conscious you can be—the quicker you will become skillful at your new activities. Emotional intensity will help neutralize fear of making mistakes, of humiliating yourself and of risking the unknown. These fears stop many adults from learning new things.

Whether your intensity comes from your indignation about what you have endured and resented for too long, or simply from wholehearted enthusiasm to try something different, strong feelings are necessary to overcome the inertia of your habitual expectations and others' expectations of you.

The capacity children have to set aside their fledging identities and lose themselves in more romantic and satisfying fantasies has a great deal to do with how quickly children learn, change and grow. Adults who emulate this childlike curiosity are those who keep growing.

The flexibility of character necessary to shed your habitual identity and its self-consciousness and immerse yourself in some new challenge requires a willingness to feel anxious and out of control while you practice new attitudes and actions. It helps to have a sense of humor about yourself. It also helps if the new behavior you've chosen also must give you more self-respect than you're accustomed to.

Alex had never put forth enthusiastic efforts at anything for fear of failure and of the expectations that would be created by success. His developing compassion helped him overcome his fear and begin for the first time to try his best.

If you're fortunate enough to have already overcome self-doubt and accepted your inherent worth, change and growth is part of your daily life. Rid of self-doubt, you no longer have to fear being revealed as defective. You don't have to be so concerned about your mistakes and how awkward you look when you're learning something new. Self-acceptance allows you to be curious and excited about discovering new aspects of yourself and the world.

"The belief that becomes truth for me . . . is that which allows me the best use of my strength, the best means of putting my virtues into action."

Andre Gide

From Self-Doubt to Self-Acceptance Summary

Self-acceptance isn't necessary for self-change. In fact, self-respect generating experiments with more compassionate and constructive attitudes are exactly what is necessary to move from self-doubt to self-acceptance. While far more challenging than changing from someone who can't type to someone who can, the leap from self-doubt to self-acceptance requires attitudes and actions similar to those necessary in any learning process.

You can't stay the same if you change how you act. If you're willing to keep playing the awkward unfamiliar role, your mistakes will decrease, the floundering of transition will disappear and you'll become who you've been trying to be. Your new identity of skier, typist or multilinguist becomes natural and your old identity seems strangely like an old friend who has gone away and would no longer fit in your life, a self you have poignant memories of but would prefer to leave behind.

You can use this same process to move from self-doubt to self-acceptance. You can't keep doubting your worth if you change how you act, how you treat yourself and how you allow yourself to be treated—as long as the changes you adopt *are* true to yourself and increase your self-respect, instead of being mere gestures to please others.

But keep in mind that it is your core sense of worth that you're trying to change, so you're in for a struggle. Self-respect generating experiments are incompatible with self-doubt and therefore far easier said than done. The Familiarity Principle will get in the way unless you're willing to put up with increased self-respect, awkwardness and discomfort.

However if you're determined, desperate or inspired enough to persist at your self-respecting actions and to maintain your warm and encouraging compassionate observer stance, you'll change. You'll learn to accept your worth, feel increasing self-respect and keep growing. Feeling compassion for your discomfort and acting in ways that increase your self-respect will turn you into a new person you're proud to accept.

Eventually your new and, at first, tentative identity will become your familiar self, The old self-critical, self-doubting identity will become a foreigner, a person who used to feel natural and real but is now inconsistent with who you actually are.

The Self-Change Attitude

In summary, the attitude necessary for self-change includes:

- *Willingness* to keep stepping back to observe your feelings, attitudes and actions

- *Faith* in yourself and *openness* to consider that you may be more than you previously believed possible

- *Imagination* and *curiosity* to think of ways you would like to change

- *Compassion* for yourself because risking the unknown is awkward and painful

- *Encouragement* from yourself to try new ways of acting

- *Excitement* about becoming a new person with greater capacities

- *Appreciation* for how good you feel about yourself when you're willing to act with self-respect despite the risks

CHAPTER 26

Self-Change: Step-By-Step

Materials Required:

a mirror and a pencil or pen.

Step One: Getting Started

A) If you began reading *Mind Traps* with this section (Part 9), you should now read chapters 1 through 10, omitting Chapter 7 for now.

B) Respond carefully to the *Childhood Questionnaire,* pp. 28–30.

C) Record all the strong feelings you notice in yourself throughout each day. Learning to discriminate between your various feelings will allow you to understand your needs and help you decide what you can do to take care of your needs and increase your self-respect. As explained in Chapter 5, *Feelings and the Human Spirit,* feelings are messages crucial to making decisions. Part 4, *Handling Feelings,* discusses key feelings and the valuable information they provide about yourself.

Merely reading and thinking about the issues and questions raised in this book is insufficient for self-change. You must put into spoken or written words what you feel and think to seriously reconsider important aspects of yourself and your life. Without conscious self-appraisal, self-change won't happen. Spaces are provided to record your responses to the questions raised in this chapter.

Step Two: The Mirror Exercise

If you want to have a better relationship with yourself, you first need to examine how you feel about yourself right now. The following *Mirror Exercise* will help you clarify your current attitudes towards yourself. You can also use it to practice the new attitudes recommended throughout the book.

One way to quickly determine how you feel about yourself is to look into your eyes in a mirror for a minute or two. Unless you can manage a long, quiet look into your own eyes and feel a sense of support and intimacy for yourself— deeply feel warmth for the vulnerable child inside that person in the mirror—then you lack self-acceptance. You suffer from self-doubt and get in the way of your own well-being.

Did you try to look in the mirror? You may be afraid to because you sense your self-doubt and don't want to face it. You can help yourself immediately and become courageous by doing the test despite your discomfort. For self-doubt to be conquered, its existence must first be recognized. Nothing is more important than to be on good terms with yourself. And you can't improve your relationship with yourself if you won't face yourself.

Practicing *The Mirror Exercise* each day is an excellent way to check on how you're feeling. You can look into your own eyes just as you look into your friends' eyes to see how they are doing. If a friend seems tense or depressed, you would care and try to be understanding. Why not be a friend to yourself and do the same?

Step Three: The Compassionate Self-Observer

This step requires you to experiment with new ways of thinking about yourself. Begin by reviewing the Self-Change Attitude described in the previous chapter (pp. 252−253). To change yourself for the better, you must be willing to stand back from yourself and adopt these positive attitudes towards yourself. You must consider the possibility that your habitual beliefs about yourself may be mistaken. You need to be willing to experiment with new priorities, attitudes and actions. If you are to change, all the remaining steps must be approached with these attitudes in mind.

To begin improving your view of yourself, think of compliments you have received. In the space below, list the positive things people who appreciate you say about you. If possible, select comments you have heard repeatedly over the years.

1.

2.

3.

4.

5.

Despite your discomfort, try seriously considering the possibility that these observations are more right about you than you are about yourself.

Step Four: Assessing Your Needs

The better each person involved in a relationship understands, cares about and helps satisfy the other person's needs, the better the relationship. The same is true in your relationship with yourself.

Chapter 24, *Well-Being: The Goal of Personal Change,* defines well-being and suggests five ingredients necessary to achieve it. You might wish to reread that chapter before proceeding.

By comparing each of the five components of well-being with your own situation, you can survey your current level of satisfaction in five important dimensions of your life.

Record your answers to the questions below regarding your current satisfaction in each of the five components. This analysis will help you to establish your goals and priorities for change.

To decrease the chance of deceiving yourself, try using a mirror and looking yourself in the eyes while answering each question. Your feelings will betray you if you try to kid yourself. Dishonest answers will cause you to squirm, avert your eyes and feel embarrassed, or perhaps even angry about having to do this exercise. Honest answers will probably stir up feelings of sadness.

Fulfillment in Work:

1. Are you confident in your inherent worth as a human being?

Do you accept that you have your strengths and weaknesses, but know there's nothing fundamentally wrong with you?

2. Are you proud of your *efforts* in your work or some other endeavor?

3. Are you concerned that what you do may not be worthwhile?

4. Consider the rewards you get for your accomplishments: Are you receiving fair and adequate financial compensation?

Appreciation?

Prestige?

Does your work seem to have a positive effect on others?

Intimacy:
Consider the important relationships in your life.

1. Are you consistently respectful towards the important people in your life?

Are they sufficiently respectful towards you?

2. Do you make an effort to understand their feelings and point of view even when you don't agree with them?

Do they do the same for you?

3. Do you freely demonstrate your love to the people you care about?

Do the people you care about accept your love?

4. Do you get and accept enough caring from others?

Personal Growth:

1. What new and challenging activities have you done recently?

2. In the space below list the ways you feel you are learning and growing:

Rest:

1. Do you take time out for relaxation? How many hours per week?

2. When was the last time you spent time relaxing?

3. What do you do for relaxation?

4. How many entire days off have you taken in the last month?

In the last year?

Recreation:

1. Do you regularly take time out to play?

2. When was the last time you played?

3. Are you usually under the influence of some intoxicant when you play?

4. What do you do for recreation?

Is it really play (not competitive and not growth-directed)?

Step Five: Creating Your Mind Trap Profile

Mind Traps, self-defeating attitudes created by self-doubt, waste time and energy and keep you stuck in familiar ruts. In order to change, you must identify your Mind Traps.

To determine your personal Mind Trap Profile, read through the *Mind Traps List,* located at the front of the book. On the chart below, in the column marked "My Initial List," check off those Mind Traps you think you may have. If you are unsure whether or not to include a particular trap in your profile, reviewing the examples and the *Commonly Associated Features* section at the beginning of the chapter devoted to that trap may help you decide.

Remember that *The Self-Doubt Trap* and *The "Bad Feelings Are Wrong" Trap* underlie all the other traps. If you have any of the other Mind Trap, you almost certainly have these basic Mind Traps, too. If you haven't included *The Self-Doubt Trap* and *The "Bad Feelings Are Wrong" Trap* in your Mind Trap Profile, review them again and consider adding them to your profile.

Show the *Mind Traps List* to two people who know you well. Ask them to write down *on a separate piece of paper* the Mind Traps they think may apply to you. Encourage them to be candid in their assessment of you, otherwise what could be an invaluable contribution becomes a meaningless waste of time.

In the columns marked "Other's Opinion," check off those Mind Traps they indicated.

Consider including in your profile those Mind Traps others have suggested. Use the column marked "Personal Mind Trap Profile" to check off your final decisions.

You may want to circle on the *Mind Traps List* each of the traps in your profile so it will be easier to refer back to them.

Although examining your Mind Traps and asking others to give their opinion of you can be disconcerting, this step is important because other people can help you see through your biases.

Couples can enhance their mutual understanding by discussing their Mind Trap Profile, as long as they avoid using the exercise to attack, blame or appease each other.

MIND TRAP PROFILE CHART

A My Initial List
B Other's Opinion (#1)
C Other's Opinion (#2)
D Personal Mind Trap Profile

MIND TRAPS	A	B	C	D
The Self-Doubt Trap				
The "Bad Feelings Are Wrong" Trap				
The "Feelings Are Foolish" Trap				
The "Biased Against Myself" Traps: a) The Compare and Despair Trap				
b) The "You Flatter Me" Trap				
The "People Don't Change" Traps: a) The "I Can't Change" Trap				
b) The "You'll Never Change" Trap				
c) The "Seen One, Seen 'Em All" Trap				
The Fear of Failure and Sucess Trap a) The Fear of Failure Trap				
b) The Fear of Success Trap				
The "There's No Use Trying" Trap				
The Blame Trap a) "I Blame Myself"				
b) "I Blame Others (or Fate or God)"				

MIND TRAPS (continued)	A	B	C	D
The "My Happiness Is Your Responsibility" Traps: a) The Dependency Trap				
b) The "Love Me And Make Me Whole" Trap				
c) The Complacent Partner Trap				
d) The Searching For the Perfect Love Trap				
The Rejection Trap: a) "Less Intimacy, Less Pain"				
b) "Better to Reject Than Be Rejected"				
c) Control the News				
The Jealousy Trap				
The Shy and Lonely Trap a) Shyness				
b) "Only Losers Are Lonely"				
The Great American Success Trap: a) Prior To Success				
b) After Success				
The Perfectionism Trap				
The Conceit Trap				
The "I'm Right and You're Wrong" Trap				
The "Your Happiness Is My Responsibility" Trap				

Step Six: Exposing Your Traps

For each of the Mind Traps in your profile, review the *Exposing the Trap* section in the chapter devoted to that trap. Briefly list the reasons you see for getting rid of each trap in your profile.

Don't skip this step. Writing may seem unnecessary and tedious, but being explicit will help you escape the traps and allow you to refer back and remind yourself of your reasons for changing.

Step Seven: Planning Your New Direction

For each of the Mind Traps in your profile, review the *New Direction* section in the chapter devoted to the trap. Underline what you feel are the essential ingredients of a new attitude you can substitute for each of the Mind Traps in your profile.

Summarize the new attitudes you can adopt to replace your Mind Traps. Explicitly writing down your new attitude will help you now and will be worth reviewing regularly. Practice is necessary to learn new attitudes.

Step Eight: Creating Your List of Possible Changes

Review your entries from Step Four and Step Seven. Keeping them in mind, think of possible changes you could make in the *ways you behave* that would give you more self-respect and a better chance at well-being.

A useful way to decide what might increase your self-respect is to imagine you're ninety years of age and looking back over your life. Which way of acting now would give you pride in yourself in the long run, even if the results were dissatisfying?

Another way of gaining perspective is to imagine that in the future you will have a child who is your current age and who happens to be in your exact situation. What change in habits would make you proudest of this child, whether or not things turned out well?

Be careful to pick *ways of acting,* not achievements and rewards. Try to be as specific as possible. How exactly would you act? What would you say and do that would be likely to make you prouder and more satisfied?

For now, consider your options merely as an idea list. You may or may not actually try any of them. Don't be concerned about examining their practicality or questioning the wisdom of carrying them out.

Record the changes you might make in the boxes labelled "Experiment" on the *Change Experiment List* (pp. 268–269).

Step Nine: Weighing the Pros and Cons

For each of these possible experiments, think of all advantages and disadvantages, best and worst possible outcomes of going ahead and trying the new ways of behaving. Enter the pros and cons in the appropriate boxes on the *Change Experiment List* below.

After weighing the pros and cons, do any of these experiments seem worth trying? If none of them are worth doing, you're not ready to change. Perhaps you need to be more desperate or more inspired before you are ready to try behaving in ways that would give you more self-respect and fulfillment.

If several of your options for change *are* worth trying, number them in order of priority in the space provided. You may want to start with smaller, easier changes first or take a dramatic leap into an entirely new way of being.

CHANGE EXPERIMENT LIST

EXPERIMENT	Priority #
Pros:	**Cons:**
Date started:	**Date someone noticed change:**

EXPERIMENT	Priority #
Pros:	**Cons:**
Date started:	**Date someone noticed change:**

EXPERIMENT	Priority #
Pros:	**Cons:**
Date started:	**Date someone noticed change:**

EXPERIMENT	Priority #
Pros:	Cons:
Date started:	Date someone noticed change:

EXPERIMENT	Priority #
Pros:	Cons:
Date started:	Date someone noticed change:

Step Ten: Getting Others to Help

People are social animals and do best in a social network. If you want to change, try to arrange for a support system. Joining a group of people who are actively working to change and grow can be an excellent way to get the encouragement you need for self-change. You can join a group organized and guided by a professional or a self-help group like the kind pioneered by Alcoholics Anonymous.

Sometimes a well-trained self-change consultant can help. Interview several therapists before deciding which one seems best. Quiz them to determine what their personal goals and values are and whether they actually live according to what they preach. Although most therapists and counselors have been trained to treat patients, you may be able to convince one of them to *coach* you instead of *treating* you. If you want to change and believe you're capable of taking primary responsibility to change yourself, then you'll do better with someone who is willing to be your consultant instead of your therapist.[1]

Whether you arrange for a formal support system or not, choose a few people you can count on to be on your side. Explain to them what, why and how you're trying to change. Describe what you'd like them to say and do to help you stay on track. Their support and encouragement will help. Also, going public will make it more embarrassing for you to surrender to the powerful pull of familiarity and return to your old ways. Self-change is your responsibility. But you'll need all the help you can get.

On the chart below, list the names of the people you might ask to support you and the support groups you might join to help you change.

NAME	Date Contacted

[1]*Please see Appendix:* Helping People Help Themselves.

Step Eleven: Start Acting Differently

It's finally time to begin carrying out some experiments. It will help to regularly rehearse your new attitudes by reading them out loud to yourself. Remember that as you go about trying out your new ways of acting you will feel excited, awkward and anxious all at the same time. If you don't feel these things you aren't really changing, you're just kidding yourself with some variation of your old habits.

If other people comment on your changes, you're doing a good job. You can record the first time someone notices each of your changes in the space provided on the *Change Experiment List*, pp. 268–269.

Step Twelve: Taking Credit and Giving Yourself Some Breaks

Expect some backsliding to old familiar ways. Keep patting yourself on the back for your courage to do the hard work and face the risks and fears involved in all self-change. Rejoice in your increased self-respect. Remember to take time out regularly from your self-change efforts to enjoy some well-deserved rest and play.

Step Thirteen: For Procastinators

You may find yourself procrastinating, unable to experiment despite having decided you want to change. Nothing could be more natural and predictable. To overcome your inertia, you may find it useful to carefully read Chapter 12, *The "People Don't Change" Traps,* and Chapter 13, *The Fear of Failure and Success Traps.* These chapters discuss many of the reasons people resist change. They may help you find the courage to face your fears and to begin to act differently.

APPENDIX

Helping People
Help Themselves

Therapy Versus Self-Change

Traditionally therapy has implied a healing process in which an expert using specialized techniques treats someone who is impaired, suffering and needs help. In therapy the person to be helped is changed under the healer's influence. Although all therapies require the active participation or at least passive cooperation of their subjects, the explicit or implied expectation and promise is that subjects will obtain relief from discomfort by cooperating with their therapists' techniques. Conventional therapies all involve this process of passive change.

Mind Traps and a previous work co-authored by this writer (*I Want To Change, But I Don't Know How*, Price Stern Sloan) are guidebooks for those who wish to take primary responsibility for changing themselves. The focus of these books is on active *self-change*, with or without the assistance of a counselor.

This begs the question: Where do therapists fit into self-change, if at all?

Therapists can play an invaluable role in the self-change enterprise if they are willing to assume a different attitude and role from that of a traditional therapist. Self-change doesn't imply refusal to seek the help of others in one's efforts to change and grow. The appropriate role of the outside helper in self-change is that of a consultant, coach or teacher, rather than that of therapist/healer.

Unlike patients or clients in traditional therapies, clients bent on self-change assume full responsibility for changing themselves. Self-change consultants can be of great service to their clients: They can provide an objective and compassionate perspective of the client's situation, offer education and advice about alternative approaches and encourage the client to persevere with the difficult, but exciting process of self-change.

Self-change consultants' expertise is based on study of the process of self-change in others and on their own ongoing experience with personal growth. To maximize their effectiveness, consultants must be open, self-disclosing models of self-change.

Goals and Presumptions of Therapy and Self-Change

Most therapies share similar goals, which may include: symptom relief; personal change (growth); increased personal responsibility; self-sufficiency; self-acceptance; compassion and respect for self and others; intimacy and meaningfulness. Self-change, with or without the assistance of a self-change consultant, is more consistent with most of these goals than is therapy.

The underlying assumptions of therapy are that the patient has a problem and needs someone else's treatment to correct it. Thus therapy has *a priori* bias that interferes with a sense of personal responsibility, self-sufficiency and self-acceptance. The bias that the patient is impaired and needs help must become an explicit focus of therapy and reversed prior to termination if patients are to feel more competent to manage their own lives and not merely relieved of their discomfort temporarily. Proper handling of termination has always been the most challenging phase of explorative psychotherapy.

Two different, fundamental assumptions underlie the self-change process. The first is that the major obstacle interfering with clients' lives is the belief that they may be inherently impaired and therefore less than worthwhile. This false premise is the faulty foundation upon which most people have constructed their lives. This fallacy must be attacked and eliminated if clients are ever to make significant, constructive changes.

The other assumption of self-change is that everyone is capable of healthier self-management and continuous growth—there's always more to learn, especially about oneself. Both self-change assumptions involve positive preconceptions about clients' capacities.

In self-change, symptoms are presumed to be the result of a complex interaction between a client's biological and psychological makeup, as determined by inheritance and experience. Self-change never looks at symptoms in isolation from a client's self-concept, coping style and life situation. Symptoms are considered to be messages worth understanding even if they cannot be entirely eliminated. Since self-change consultants can't and don't promise elimination of symptoms, clients can't use their symptoms to hide from themselves and their situations. Clients are continually encouraged to step back from themselves to compassionately reconsider their past and current situation to come up with potentially better ways of seeing themselves and of handling their lives. The self-change credo is:

Change yourself for the better and you'll get (some) symptom relief along with greater satisfaction of the other ingredients necessary for well-being.

Complete relief often isn't possible. In the futile pursuit of therapeutic magic, life can deteriorate into a desperate dependency on healers to find a cure.

Self-change clients come to consultants not *to be healed* of their problems, but to enhance their skills in the *art of living.* Self-change clients never relinquish personal responsibility in the process of enhancing their self-sufficiency, achieving self-acceptance and finding the maximum possible relief for their symptoms.

Although self-change never allows symptoms to be the primary or exclusive focus, the self-change orientation of a consultation doesn't preclude the occasional use of specialized techniques (behavior modification, medication, hypnosis) for symptom relief. These techniques can be provided by the self-change consultant or some other expert if they are requested by a client who has been apprised of the risks and benefits of the alternatives available. But symptom-directed passive change approaches are employed only as a supplement to the self-change process once it is already successfully underway.

A challenge for the self-change consultant is to maintain continuous pressure on their clients to accept responsibility for experimenting with attitudes and actions in between sessions so the clients can become increasingly proficient at arranging for their own (spiritual) well-being. However well-intentioned and motivated for self-change the client is, the familiar self invariably resists giving way to the compassionate observer within who must quarterback the self-change. One way the self-doubting familiar self can interfere with change and growth is by influencing the consultant to become a symptom-preoccupied caretaking therapist. The consultant must try to maintain the stance of a coach who cares and wants to teach clients how to improve their ability to take care of themselves and to achieve self-acceptance.

Paradoxes of Therapy and Self-Change

Therapy and self-change both must resolve a paradox if they are to be effective in accomplishing change. But the paradox is different in each. The paradox in therapy is that patients eventually must learn to take better *care of themselves* while *under the care of* a therapist. The difficulty caused by this paradox is that patients often become more proficient at being dependent on and cared for by their therapists then at taking better care of themselves.

The self-change paradox is: Who is the person who changes the person who changes? The difficulty in self-change caused by this paradox is the resistance of the familiar identity to compassionate reappraisal and to yielding its long-standing control over the client's life.

Advantages of Self-Change

Many potential advantages accrue to those who choose to embark on coached self-change instead of therapy-induced change.

Therapists traditionally have hidden themselves from patients/clients behind facades—from a blank screen to an arm's length professional manner. These facades prevent therapists from freely offering their full experience and from openly expressing their enthusiastic support to patients. This deprives the therapeutic partnership of its most powerful resources.

Artificial therapeutic stances are pretenses that imply the therapist's life is always under control and going beautifully. These facades have been necessary because some blind faith is required if patients are to completely place responsibility for their psychological well-being in the hands of therapists. Unfortunately, the suicide, alcoholism and addiction rates, sexual transgressions and other personal life problems of many highly trained therapists have been too highly publicized to maintain the illusion that therapists are privy to some form of higher consciousness and well-being. Quite the opposite is true. Our field attracts and provides a living to many wounded and vulnerable people who make the best and worst of therapists. No amount of training and previous therapy is a substitute for self-acceptance, self-respect and continuing growth.

Self-change consultants needn't adopt any poses. If consultants are willing to admit their human frailities and vulnerabilities, they can be much more helpful to their clients. When a self-disclosure is relevant to the client's current issues, self-change consultants can divulge information about their own struggles for self-respect and well-being. In this way, consultants bring an important advantage of peer and group counseling into the self-change consultation.

Consultants have the responsibility of practicing in their private lives what they proselytize in their offices and then to introduce that experience into their sessions with clients. Self-change consultants must take excellent care of themselves because they are continually revealing themselves to their clients.

Because self-change consultants are themselves committed to the noble pursuit of mastering the art of living, they can relate to clients in a natural, "we're all in this together," supportive and encouraging manner. They can be active and enthusiastic participants in their consultations, instead of reserved and private priestlike therapists pretending to live on a more saintly plane and thus in a privileged position to assist their mere mortal patients. Instead of a contrived, sharply defined hierarchal relationship between therapist and client, the consultant-client relationship in self-change can be a forum for the practice of healthy person-to-person communication.

Like everyone else, self-change consultants are challenged to live the best they can. Yet, self-change consultants are also professionals who devote their lives to the study of personal growth and the art of living. They offer the benefits of their accumulated wisdom to clients pursuing the same goals.

Clients are in a position to take the initiative occasionally and be helpful to their consultants. All this open exchange can take place without losing sight of the fact that consultants are there to serve their clients' interests not their own. The same ethical standards apply to self-change consultations as therapy, but in a more honest, less contrived atmosphere. The less artificial the learning environment, the more readily its lessons can be applied to everyday life.

The medical model upon which all therapies are based promises too much, delivers too little and absolves patients of the responsibility to optimize their own lives. This is a serious disadvantage. Personal responsibility is the best weapon clients have in their quest for well-being.

The self-change consultation philosophy offers less and delivers more: Experts are consulted to help out, not to take over responsibility for one's own welfare. No one is defective. Everyone is responsibly and courageously trying to do the best one can with what one has available—from those ill with cancer or multiple sclerosis, schizophrenia or manic-depressive disorders, to healthy young adults wanting to overcome their fear of success and failure, or couples struggling to find more intimacy. No one else can make people feel good about themselves. But an outside person can help by offering advice, observations and inspiration.

Limitations on Self-Change

Self-change has limitations beyond the self-changing-self paradox. Of the various elements distinguishable in one's own mental life—needs, desires, beliefs, feelings, perceptions, bodily sensations, thoughts, memories, will, attitudes and actions—one can only deliberately and consistently exert control over *attitudes* and *actions*. For example, I can't decide at any moment to change my religious beliefs or change my perception of the chair I'm sitting on and begin to see it, feel it and believe it to be the branch of a tree. And, despite the claims of pop psychology, I can't simply *choose* not to feel hurt and sad when my best friend dies. Similarly, I can't always decide what to think, remember, desire and so forth. So self-change must exclusively rely on willfully adopted attitudes and actions to accomplish its end—self-initiated, self-directed change and growth.

Fortunately, changes in attitude and action alone are enough to accomplish self-change. One can predictably and deliberately *choose* to act *as if* one thinks, feels, believes, desires or perceives something—however inauthentic one knows those attitudes and actions to be. One can decide to artificially adopt a particular attitude and action. One can maintain this act despite any awkwardness and anxiety one might feel about acting in unfamiliar ways.

If one's affectation is consistent with what would increase self-respect and better fulfill needs than were one's habitual attitudes and actions, and if one keeps up this noble charade long enough to loosen the grip of one's familiar identity, then one will change. By persisting at novel, self-respecting and compassionate attitudes and actions despite awkwardness and fear, eventually one will see and feel different and better than one has ever been. A new identity will take over and one will have changed in the most profound sense.

Compassion requires courageous self-observation (despite fear of confronting one's sense of defectiveness). Self-respect requires courageous experimentation (despite fear of failure, success and rejection). Consultants can't give their clients courage, but they can inspire them by modeling it.

Even after one has begun to make efforts at change, one must have a great deal of motivation to persist at self-change. Resistance to self-change comes from awkwardness and from fear of losing one's habitual identity, of facing the unknown and of taking the responsibility to be in charge of one's own life. Fear caused by self-change can sometimes even reach the point of terror. However, the pay-off for those who persist is the freedom to be the best they can be.

Brainwashing and the Limitations of Conventional Therapies

Increased understanding of coercive influence ("mind control," "brainwashing") over the past thirty years has made traditional methods of therapeutic influence obsolete. Coercive influence as practiced by governments, terrorists and various cults has been convincingly successful at influencing the minds and actions of their victims. Long-standing changes are produced in a relatively short period of time.

Sports psychologists in Eastern Bloc countries and, more recently, in the West, have adapted mind control techniques to successfully enhance athletes' performance. In locations like the U.S. Olympic Team's training facilities at Colorado Springs, athletes are sequestered for prolonged periods in relatively controlled environments. In these training centers, the athletes' activities, dress, daily habits and other aspects of their lives can be controlled by their coaches. In this way the athletes' minds and bodies can be programmed to maximize their performances. (Of course, the athletes subject themselves to this treatment voluntarily.)

The influencing techniques practiced by conventional therapists with patients are lame in comparison to those available to these athletic coaches, cult and political indoctrinators, who have greater control over the daily lives of their subjects.

Therapists who wish to continue to act as therapist-influencers instead of self-change consultants would do well to consider creating similar therapeutic environments. In controlled isolated facilities (referred to as "Intensive Change Centers," perhaps), people wishing to be influenced to attain specified goals would come voluntarily for several weeks and be subjected with their informed consent to established mind control techniques. Monasteries and the Marine Corps provide an indication of what such centers might be capable of accomplishing with their subjects. A watered-down mind control approach in the health care industry is already well-established in the form of voluntarily in-patient treatment programs for substance abuse and eating disorders.[1]

People would arrive at Intensive Change Centers having already worked out their personal goals with their private consultants. Once a person was admitted to a center, trainers would take over every aspect of the subject's life for a predetermined period of time. Although a subject's initial participation would be completely voluntary, they would yield the right to leave the program until and unless they have given twenty-four hours written notice of their intent to stop being influenced. Prior to admission they would have been educated to the likelihood of a positive identity crisis with its attendant anxiety, confusion and desire to escape.

The subject's private consultant would visit regularly and be the only outside person with whom contact would be allowed, at least during an initial time period. The centers would be licensed, regulated and monitored by the state. Private consultants would be available to clients for follow-up after discharge. To prevent conflict of interest, these consultants would not receive any referrals or financial remuneration from the intensive change centers.

Intensive Change Centers would be ethical and allow the

[1]*More than any other modern therapy, Janov's Primal Scream Therapy makes use of mind control tactics by isolating clients for several weeks from any contact with the outside world other than daily sessions with the therapist.*

use of far more effective and efficient influencing techniques than the relatively weak interventions currently employed by conventional therapists. A person wishing to change would then have some clear choices: Embark on self-change with or without a consultant to coach you while you remain in control of your life, or give yourself over to experts at mind control and achieve *your* goals far more efficiently. In other words, if you want to be passively changed, go all out and have other people do it as efficiently as possible. Or else, take matters in your own hands and, with or without the help of a consultant, change yourself.

Self-Change—A Conceptual Framework

From cognitive therapy to psychoanalysis, each approach to therapy is based on observations made by therapists that have been summarized and concretized into a model. Patients (clients) eventually learn to label their experiences according to the symbol system and framework employed by their therapists. This labeling process and the theory connecting these labeled experiences can be immensely nelpful in the change process.

If self-change is to be effective and distinct from being changed by therapy, self-change requires its own model. This model must be couched (if you'll excuse the expression) in language that is accessible to clients and consultants. Self-change consultants can't have a language distinct from that used by their clients. If experts speak in their own language, they create a hierarchy with themselves above (clergy) and clients (laity) below. The use of inaccessible, technical terms would subvert the entire self-change enterprise.

Emerging from one's habitual, experiential rut is the major challenge of self-change. It is difficult to get a grip on oneself The key to effective self-influence is to take sufficient distance to allow for compassion or at least objectivity. Hence the value of models. So self-change theory should combine experiential (especially affectual), intellectual, behavioral and developmental perspectives to give people as many different handles on themselves as possible.

Over the course of this book I have described a conceptual framework that might be called the "Identity Familiarity and Crisis Theory." It is a cognitive, behavioral, developmental and, above all, experiential model for self-change.

The Identity Familiarity and Crisis Theory emphasizes, labels and defines phenomena that are recognizable in everyone's conscious experience. Little attention is given either to differentiating conscious from unconscious processes or to interpreting the symbolism characteristic of unconscious thinking, dreams and artistic creation.

Unconscious mental activity is by definition out of awareness. Theories and approaches that emphasize unconscious processes usually require a therapist-interpreter and tend to discourage personal initiative and responsibility for attitudes and actions. This emphasis on conscious experience doesn't mean the unconscious is forbidden or inaccessible to people embarked on self-change. Techniques are available to enhance creativity through increased awareness of one's own unconscious symbolic activity through such things as self-analysis of dreams, a variety of so-called "right-brain" exercises and guided imagery.

Identity Familiarity & Crisis Theory (in brief)

Diagram I is an attempt to capture in graphic form the relationship of some of the theory's central elements. Each of the key concepts in the diagram are defined in the *Glossary,* pp. 291–293. The diagram depicts a hypothetical "Person A" trapped in a familiar self-doubting identity, caught between the fear of either a negative or positive identity crisis.

DIAGRAM I: IDENTITY FAMILIARITY AND CRISIS THEORY

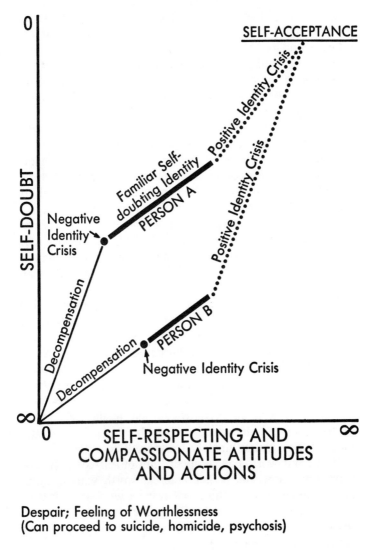

Despair; Feeling of Worthlessness
(Can proceed to suicide, homicide, psychosis)

Self-doubt makes a person especially vulnerable to whatever that person perceives is a rejection, loss or failure. Any or all of these cause a *negative identity crisis* and decompensation into a sense of worthlessness and despair (with the potential for psychosis, suicide and homicide). At the upper boundary of the person's familiar identity, a frightening and awkward *positive identity crisis* would ensue if the person were to act and be treated in unfamiliar respectful and compassionate ways for a prolonged period (*The Familiarity Principle*).

Diagram I shows that the antithesis of self-doubt is self-acceptance. (High self-esteem is a mirage, a compensatory defense against self-doubt. Self-acceptance is the pinnacle of self-worth.) Self-doubt reflects the danger and fear of feeling worthless. But self-acceptance, once achieved, is absolute protection from further doubt about one's inherent worth. (On the diagram, the self-acceptance line is discontinuous with that of the familiar self-doubting identity.) Of course, self-acceptance is no protection against the hurt of loss, rejection and failure or the challenging struggle with insoluble existential dilemmas.

Diagram I also indicates the theory's differentiation between self-worth and self-respect and the relationship between the two. Self-respect must be earned by honest efforts. Self-acceptance (absence of self-doubt) is an unprovable belief which can be acquired by adopting compassionate and respectful attitudes (*Escape Routes* from *Mind Traps*). The more Person A acts with self-respect and compassion the more he moves up and to the right in the diagram, toward decreased self-doubt, toward a positive identity crisis and, ultimately, toward self-acceptance.

While self-worth has an upper limit of self-acceptance— a person accepts his or her inherent worth without question—you can keep earning self-respect without limit once self-acceptance is attained. (Of course, you can lose self-respect whenever you act like a jerk even if you have achieved self-acceptance.)

Prior to self-acceptance, self-respectful and compassionate attitudes and actions are limited by the threat of a positive identity crisis. The absence of any established path in Diagram I from the familiar identity to self-acceptance implies the terrifying void of the unknown that confronts self-doubting people who wish to learn to accept themselves. To be able to accept themselves, they have to choose to become substantially different (more compassionate and respectful of self and others) than they have ever been.

The short and steep line labeled "Person B" below Person A on the left descending slope indicates the narrower range between positive and negative crises and the difficulty avoiding repetitive negative crises for people with more severe self-doubt (greater childhood wounds). That is, people with severe self-doubt have more rigid personalities and are more susceptible to crises. The large gap between self-acceptance and the upper limit of Person B's familiar identity suggests what feels like a terrifyingly impossible hurdle for many severely wounded people (so-called "narcissistic" and "borderline" personalities). To change is to risk disappearing into the void and ceasing to exist, in the psychological sense. For many, suicide is easier.

Diagram II depicts the self-change process from self-doubt to self-acceptance. The difficult process of deliberate self-change is indicated by the short thick arrows. The longer, slender arrows trace the more common detour, despite one's best intentions, along the path of least resistance back to habitual Mind Traps and to one's familiar, self-doubting identity.

Neither diagram incorporates the crucial role of feelings as coded messages that must be deciphered if one is to attain self-acceptance and the reversal of alienation from the true self.[2]

---

[2]*Discussed in Parts 2, 3 and 4 of* Mind Traps.

DIAGRAM II: CHANGE AND RESISTANCE TO CHANGE (IDENTITY FAMILIARITY AND CRISIS THEORY)

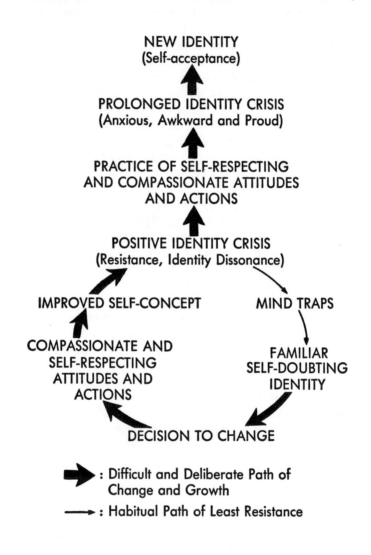

NEW IDENTITY
(Self-acceptance)

PROLONGED IDENTITY CRISIS
(Anxious, Awkward and Proud)

PRACTICE OF SELF-RESPECTING
AND COMPASSIONATE ATTITUDES
AND ACTIONS

POSITIVE IDENTITY CRISIS
(Resistance, Identity Dissonance)

IMPROVED SELF-CONCEPT

MIND TRAPS

COMPASSIONATE AND
SELF-RESPECTING
ATTITUDES AND
ACTIONS

FAMILIAR
SELF-DOUBTING
IDENTITY

DECISION TO CHANGE

: Difficult and Deliberate Path of
Change and Growth

: Habitual Path of Least Resistance

Any theory that attempts to incorporate all of human experience and behavior becomes complicated beyond practical application. The theory and approach described in this book is designed specifically to facilitate self-change by concentrating on conscious mental phenomena accessible to direct monitoring and influence by oneself, of oneself.

I believe traditional modes of therapy as practiced currently in therapists' offices will prove to be less effective, efficient and acceptable to consumers than self-change with or without self-change consultations. I hope *Mind Traps* and my previous book, *I Want To Change, But I Don't Know How,* will contribute to that future.

Glossary

This glossary defines key words and phrases as they are used in *Mind Traps.* The glossary contains definitions of all italicized words.

Compassionate Self-Observer: The part of one's mind that can stand back and observe one's own actions and feelings with an encouraging and comforting bias. The *Compassionate Self-Observer* allows one to conceive of and carry out self-change.

Escape Route: A healthy alternative to a *Mind Trap;* an attitude more likely to produce *self-acceptance* and *well-being.*

Familiarity Principle: The dictum that people will act in ways that are familiar even if those ways are not in their best interest.

Familiar Self: The *identity* one is accustomed to, primarily established in childhood but developed throughout life. Also called the habitual self.

Human Spirit: The inherent nature and potentials of an individual; a person's unique hereditary endowment of energy, needs, talents, sensitivities and will. The source of feelings. (Used synonymously with *true self.* Although not identical to the *inner child,* the terms are used interchangeably in this book.)

Identity: One's sense of self, including one's habits, the way one views oneself and the way one is accustomed to feeling.

Identity Crisis: A threat to one's *familiar self.* An *identity crisis* always causes discomfort but can be positive or negative in its effects. (See also *Positive Identity Crisis* and *Negative Identity Crisis.*)

Inner Child: The vulnerable part of oneself which needs comforting, love and play. The *inner child* is wounded by uncomforted pain in childhood and persists as a powerful influence throughout life.

Mind Traps: Self-defeating attitudes. There are three major types of *Mind Traps*:
1. attempts to compensate for *self-doubt* and avoid a *negative identity crisis*;
2. attempts to maintain one's familiar self-doubting identity and prevent a *positive identity crisis.*
3. *attempts to avoid situations that might lead to failure, loss or rejection.*

Mind Trap Profile: An individual's particular set of *Mind Traps.*

Negative Identity Crisis: Fear of worthlessness precipitated in self-doubting people by rejection, loss or failure.

Observing Self: That part of consciousness capable of self-awareness. The *observing self* can monitor experience while one is engaged in some activity; may vary in perspective from self-critical self-consciousness to objectivity to compassionate self-awareness.

Positive Identity Crisis: Acute discomfort because of a threat to one's *familiar self* caused by any change which increases one's *self-respect* and compassion for self and others.

Self-Acceptance: Certainty about one's own inherent worth; the absence of *self-doubt.*

Self-Doubt: Concern that one may be defective in some

fundamental and perhaps irreversible way. *Self-doubt* may be hidden behind other Mind Traps, like *The Conceit Trap, The Blame Trap* and *The "Feelings Are Foolish" Trap.*

Self-Respect: A positive feeling about oneself earned by acting in accord with one's own sense of what is right. Requires difficult or frightening efforts to accomplish something one believes is worthwhile. Given an endeavor one deems is worthy, the greater the challenge, the greater the self-respect. Not to be confused with feeling approved of because of obedience to external expectations or with the pleasure one feels when various needs (hunger, sex, sleep) are satisfied.

Sense of Worth: One's feeling about oneself; a core part of one's *identity*; can range from worthlessness and self-hatred to *self-acceptance,* but varies little in a single individual over time. Established in childhood.

True Self: Opposite of false, self-doubting self. Used synonymously with *human spirit.*

Well-Being: An ideal state in which one experiences *self-acceptance* along with satisfaction of basic physical needs and of the needs for fulfillment in work, intimacy in relationships, personal growth and regular rest and recreation.

INDEX

THE SELF-CHANGE *SOFTWARE* PROGRAM

A fascinating new way to achieve lasting change!
The Self-Change Software Program will help you:

* discover what may be missing in your life
* sort out your feelings
* uncover self-defeating attitudes
* adopt new ways of thinking
* choose experiments that will bring you self-acceptance and well-being

The Self-Change Software Program asks you **seven** detailed series of questions. It analyzes your responses and uses this analysis to guide you step-by-step through a personalized self-change program. Included is an option to obtain other people's opinions about your attitudes.

Priced at $49.95, the Self-Change Software Package contains the software program (not copy protected), documentation and a copy of *MIND TRAPS: Change Your Mind/Change Your Life*. No computer experience necessary.

To order, send in form on other side or call (619) 280-0333, M-Th. 10-4 PM PT.

For IBM and compatibles, 384K Memory, DOS 2.0 or higher. (Price subject to change.)

DATE DUE	BORROWER'S NAME	ROOM NUMBER
JAN 15 '90	Dick Reinisch fac	
AUG 23 '9?	Renew	
JUN 8 '92	Renew	
AUG 26 '94	Renew	
AUG 26 '94	Mark Mal Malin	
JUN 05 '95		
JUL 08 '0?	D	